Building Wealth

THE BENEFITS OF BEING A RESIDENTIAL REAL ESTATE
INVESTOR: DON'T GET RICH QUICK, GET RICH FOR SURE!

BY:

Steve Alkandros

TABLE OF CONTENTS

INTRODUCTION..3

CHAPTER ONE..5

    Real Estate Investing Guide for New Investors..................................5

    WHTAT IS REAL ESTATE AND How to Invest in Real Estate...............8

    Residential Real Estate Investing - Is Residential Real Estate Investing The Best Way To Make Money?..22

    Factors That Influence Investing In Residential Real Estate.............33

    How to Prepare Yourself to Meet and Capture Real Estate Investors 46

CHAPTER TWO..48

    Starting a Business in Residential Real Estate Investing..................49

    9 Ways To Invest In Real Estate Without Buying Property...............52

    The Benefits Of Investing In Residential Real Estate........................84

    The Benefits Of Investing In Real Estate Vs. Other Investment Opportunities..94

    The Incredible Tax Benefits of Real Estate Investing......................100

CHAPTER THREE..111

10 Habits of Successful Real Estate Investors..................................111

8 Pitfalls to Avoid When Investing in Residential Real Estate.........116

6 Advantages of Real Estate Investing for Savvy Entrepreneurs....123

The advantages of investing in commercial real estate today........126

CHAPTER FOUR...131

How Real Estate Investments Return Profits..................................132

35 reasons to invest in real estate..134

3 Most Profitable Types of Real Estate Investment.......................151

CONCLUSION...155

INTRODUCTION

Residential real estate investing is a business activity that has waxed and waned in popularity dramatically over the last few years. Ironically, there always seem to be a lot of people jumping on board with investments like stock, gold, and real estate when the market's going up, and jumping OFF the wagon and pursuing other activities once the market's slumping. In a way that's human nature, but it also means a lot of real estate investors are leaving money on the table. By understanding the dynamics of your residential real estate investment marketplace, and acting in opposition to the rest of the market, you can often make more money, as long as you also stick to the real estate investing fundamentals. Real estate investing, whether you're buying residential or commercial property, is not a get-rich-quick scenario. Sure you can make some fast cash flipping houses, if that's your bag, but that is a full time business activity, not a passive, long term investment. The word "investment" implies that you are committed to the activity for the long haul. Often, that's just what it takes to make money in real estate. So, while the pundits are crying about the residential real estate market slump, and the speculators are wondering if this is the bottom, let us return to the fundamentals of residential real estate investing, and learn how to make money investing in real estate for the long term, in good markets, as well as bad. Residential real estate investing is something that's incredibly simple and complex at the same time. At the conceptual level, we all understand the end goal of buying property, letting it appreciate over time, and cashing out at a later date.

CHAPTER ONE

REAL ESTATE INVESTING GUIDE FOR NEW INVESTORS

For many people, real estate is the easiest to understand investment because it is simple, straight-forward and involves a fair exchange between a property owner (the landlord) and the property user (the renter). As long as the hot water keeps flowing and the rent arrives on time, everyone is happy and benefits. Investing in real estate is much more complex than this, though, because there are several different types of real estate investments including residential, commercial, and industrial, as well as real estate that trades on stock exchanges, which are called REITs. This guide was designed to help you.

Real Estate Investing for Beginners

When you invest in real estate, your goal is to put money to work today and make it grow so you have more money in the future. You have to make enough profit, or "return", to cover the risk you take, taxes you pay, and the costs of owning the real estate investment such as utilities and insurance. This overview explains the basics of real estate investing for beginners to help you learn what to expect and how investors make money from their real estate properties.

The 8 Different Types of Real Estate Investments

There are eight different types of real estate investments that new investors need to understand: Commercial real estate, residential real estate, industrial real estate, mixed-use real estate, retail real estate, REITs, mortgage lending, and sale/leaseback transactions. Each has its own benefits and drawbacks.

This basic guide gives you a brief explanation so you won't be intimidated or overwhelmed when you are examining potential investments and see the terms used. There are additional types of property, including multi-generational real estate. Learn the eight types of real estate investment.

Where Is the Best Place to Invest My Down Payment Money?

If you are considering buying real estate, whether it is a primary residence for your family or an investment property, you need to know how to keep your downpayment money safe and easily accessible. Here are some ideas for the best places to invest your down payment money...

Which Is Better - Real Estate or Stocks?

As a new investor, do you ever wonder which is better: stocks or real estate? Both have certain advantages and drawbacks but the answer may depend just as much on your personality and tastes as it does your portfolio and situation. Find out which investment may be a wiser choice.

What are REITs? Are They Better Than Buying Property Directly?

One of the most popular ways to own real estate is through a special type of investment known as a REIT, which is short for real estate investment trust. Real estate investment trusts come in nearly-limitless "flavors" - for example, some invest only in commercial real estate, and others only in apartment complexes. You can trade REITs just like stocks through a brokerage account and the dividends are taxed differently than dividends from stocks. Discover how REITs work and whether you should consider owning them instead of direct real estate property...

Should You Pay Off the Mortgage on Your Real Estate Early?

Some financial advisers will tell you to send extra payments to your creditor to lower your real estate debt. Others will tell you to keep more money on hand instead, so you can stockpile a decently sized emergency fund. Which is correct? Here are some things to consider, especially if you don' have enough liquidity on hand to avoid financial danger.

Using LLCs to Own Your Real Estate Investments for Risk Management

You should almost never, under any condition, own a real estate investment directly in your own name! Most of the time, serious real estate investors own properties through something known as a limited liability company or LLC. These special types of companies can protect your personal assets from lawsuits and other dangers. In fact, most wealthy investors own their home through an LLC as a risk management practice. As a potential new real estate investor, it is imperative that you understand how LLCs work and why you may want to use them to hold your rental properties or other real estate investments.

The Great Real Estate Myth

One of the biggest investments someone will make in their life is their primary residence. Unfortunately, few new investors/homeowners realize that once you factor in the cost of insurance, maintenance, net interest costs on the mortgage and other expenses, your real rate of return after inflation on a home is roughly 0%. That doesn't have to be the case, but you should go into your first major real estate investment with your eyes wide open. Here is what you need to know about the great real estate myth.

WHTAT IS REAL ESTATE AND HOW TO INVEST IN REAL ESTATE

Investing in real estate is one of the oldest forms of investing, having been around since the early days of human civilization. Predating modern stock markets, real estate is one of the five basic asset classes that every investor should seriously consider adding to his or her portfolio for the unique cash flow, liquidity, profitability, tax, and diversification benefits it offers. In this introductory guide, we'll walk you through the basics of real estate investing, and discuss the different ways you might acquire or take ownership in real estate investments.

First, let's start with the basics: What is real estate investing?

What Is Real Estate Investing?

Real estate investing is a broad category of operating, investing, and financial activities centered around making money from tangible property or cash flows somehow tied to a tangible property.

There are four main ways to make money in real estate:

Real Estate Appreciation: This is when the property increases in value. This may be due to a change in the real estate market that increases demand for property in your area. It could use be due to upgrades you put into your real estate investment to make it more attractive to potential buyers or renters. Real estate appreciation is a tricky game, though.

Cash Flow Income (Rent): This type of real estate investment focuses on buying a real estate property, such as an apartment building, and operating it so you collect a stream of cash from rent. Cash flow income can be generated from apartment buildings, office buildings, rental houses, and more.

Real Estate Related Income: This is income generated by brokers and other industry specialists who make money through commissions from buying and selling property. It also includes real estate management companies who get to keep a percentage of rents in exchange for running the day-to-day operations of a property.

Ancillary Real Estate Investment Income: For some real estate investments, this can be a huge source of profit. Ancillary real estate investment income includes things like vending machines in office buildings or laundry facilities in low-rent apartments. In effect, they serve as mini-businesses within a bigger real estate investment, letting you make money from a semi-captive collection of customers.

The purest, simplest form of real estate investing is all about cash flow from rents rather than appreciation. Real estate investing occurs when the investor, also known as the landlord, acquires a piece of tangible property, whether that's raw farmland, land with a house on it, land with an office building on it, land with an industrial warehouse on it, or an apartment.

He or she then finds someone who wants to use this property, known as a tenant, and they enter into an agreement. The tenant is granted access to the real estate, to use it under certain terms, for a specific length of time, and with certain restrictions -- some of which are laid out in Federal, state, and local law, and others of which are agreed upon in the lease contract or rental agreement. In exchange, the tenant pays for the ability to use the real estate. The payment he or she sends to the landlord is known as "rent".

For many investors, rental income from real estate investments has a huge psychological advantage over dividends and interest from investing in stocks and bonds. They can drive by the property, see it, and touch it with their hands. They can paint it their favorite color or hire an architect and construction company to modify it. They can use their negotiation skills to determine the rental rate, allowing a good operator to generate higher capitalization rates, or "cap rates."

From time to time, real estate investors become as misguided as stock investors during stock market bubbles, insisting that capitalization rates don't matter. Don't fall for it. If you are able to price your rental rates appropriately, you should enjoy a satisfactory rate of return on your capital after accounting for the cost of the property, including reasonable depreciation reserves, property and income taxes, maintenance, insurance, and other related expenditures. Additionally, you should measure the amount of time required to deal with the investment, as your time is the most valuable asset you have -- it's the reason passive income is so cherished by investors. (Once your holdings are large enough, you can establish or hire a real estate property management company to handle the day-to-day operations of your real estate portfolio in exchange for a percentage of the rental revenue, transforming real estate investments that had been actively managed into passive investments.)

What Are Some of the Most Popular Ways for a Person to Begin Investing in Real Estate?

There is a myriad of different types of real estate investments a person might consider for his or her portfolio.

It's easier to think in terms of the major categories into which real estate investments fall based on the unique benefits and drawbacks, economic characteristics and rent cycles, customary lease terms, and brokerage practices of the property type. Real estate properties are ordinarily categorized into one of the following groups:

Residential real estate investing - These are properties that involve investing in real estate tied to houses or apartments in which individuals or families live. Sometimes, real estate investments of this type have a service business component, such as assisted living facilities for seniors or full-service buildings for tenants who want a luxury experience. Leases usually run for 12 months, give or take six months on either side, leading to a much more rapid adjustment to market conditions than certain other types of real estate investments.

Commercial real estate investing - Commercial real estate investments largely consist of office buildings. These leases can be locked in for many years, resulting in a double-edged sword. When a commercial real estate investment is fully leased with long-term tenants who agreed to richly priced lease rates, the cash flow continues even if the lease rates on comparable properties fall (provided the tenant doesn't go bankrupt). On the other hand, the opposite is true - you could find yourself earning significantly below-market lease rates on an office building because you signed long-term leases before lease rates increased.

Industrial real estate investing - Properties that fall under the industrial real estate umbrella can include warehouses and distribution centers, storage units, manufacturing facilities, and assembly plants.

Retail real estate investing - Some investors want to own properties such as shopping centers, strip malls, or traditional malls. Tenants can include retail shops, hair salons, restaurants, and similar enterprises. In some cases, rental rates include a percentage of a store's retail sales to create an incentive for the landlord to do as much as he, she, or it can to make the retail property attractive to shoppers.

Mixed-use real estate investing - This is a catch-all category for when an investor develops or acquires a property that includes multiple types of the aforementioned real estate investments. For example, you might build a multi-story building that has retail and restaurants on the ground floor, office space on the next few floors, and residential apartments on the remaining floors.

You can also get involved on the lending side of real estate investing by:

Owning a bank that underwrites mortgages and commercial real estate loans. This can include public ownership of stocks. When an institutional or individual investor is analyzing a bank stocks, it pays to pay attention to the real estate exposure of the bank loans.

Underwriting private mortgages for individuals, often at higher interest rates to compensate you for the additional risk, perhaps including a lease-to-own credit provision.

Investing in mezzanine securities, which allows you to lend money to a real estate project that you can then convert into equity ownership if it isn't repaid. These are sometimes used in the development of hotel franchises.

There are sub-specialties of real estate investing including:

Leasing a space so you have little capital tied up in it, improving it, then sub-leasing that same space to others for much higher rates, creating incredible returns on capital. An example is a well-run flexible office business in a major city where smaller or mobile workers can buy office time or rent specific offices.

Acquiring tax-lien certificates. These are an esoteric area of real estate investing and not appropriate for hands-off or inexperienced investors but which -- under the right circumstances, at the right time, and with the right sort of person -- generate high returns to compensate for the headaches and risks involved.

Real Estate Investment Trusts (REITs)

On top of all of this, you can actually invest in real estate through something known as a real estate investment trust, or REIT. An investor can buy REITs through a brokerage account, Roth IRA, or another custody account of some sort. REITs are unique because the tax structure under which they are operated was created back during the Eisenhower administration to encourage smaller investors to invest in real estate projects they otherwise wouldn't be able to afford, such as building shopping centers or hotels. Corporations that have opted for REIT treatment pay no Federal income tax on their corporate earnings as long as they follow a few rules, including a requirement to distribute 90% or more of profits to shareholders as dividends.

One downside of investing in REITs is that, unlike common stocks, the dividends paid out on them are not "qualified dividends", meaning the owner can't take advantage of the low tax rates available for most dividends. Instead, dividends from real estate investment trusts are taxed at the investor's personal rate. On the upside, the IRS has subsequently ruled that REIT dividends generated within a tax shelter such as a Rollover IRA are largely not subject to the unrelated business income tax so you might be able to hold them in a retirement account without much worry of tax complexity, unlike a master limited partnership.

(If you're interested in learning more about these unique securities, start by checking out Real Estate Investing Through REITs, which covers REIT liquidity, equity, how to use REITs to your real estate investing advantage, and much more.)

Investing in Real Estate Through Home Ownership

For all the real estate investing options available to investors, the average person is going to get his or her first real estate ownership experience the traditional way: By purchasing a home.

I've never viewed the acquisition of a home quite the same way most of society does. Instead, think of a person's primary residence as a blend of personal utility and financial valuation, and not necessarily an investment. To be more direct, a home isn't an investment in the same way an apartment building is. At its very best, and under the most ideal of circumstances, the safest strategy is to think of a home as a type of forced savings account that gives you a lot of personal use and joy while you reside in it.

On the other hand, as you approach retirement, if you take a holistic view of your personal wealth, outright ownership of a home (without any debt against it) is one of the best investments a person can make. Not only can the equity be tapped through the use of certain transactions, including reverse mortgages, but the cash flow saved from not having to rent generally results in net savings -- the profit component that would have gone to the landlord effectively stays in the homeowner's pocket. This effect is so powerful that even back in the 1920s economists were trying to figure out a way for the Federal government to tax the cash savings over renting for debt-free homeowners, considering it a source of income.

This is a different type of investment, though -- something known as a "strategic investment." Were the economy to collapse, as long as you could pay the property taxes and basic upkeep, no one could evict you from your home. Even if you had to grow your own food in a garden, there's a level of personal safety there that matters. There are times when financial returns are secondary to other, more practical considerations. Whatever you do, though, don't sacrifice your liquidity to try and build equity in your real estate investments too quickly, as that can lead to disaster (including bankruptcy).

If you are saving to acquire a home, one of the big mistakes I see is new investors putting their money into the stock market, either through individual stocks or index funds. If you have any chance of needing to tap your money within five years or less, you have no business being anywhere near the stock market. Instead, you should be following an investment mandate known as capital preservation. Here are the best places to invest money you're saving for a down payment.

Which Is Better - Real Estate Investing or Investing in Stocks?

One of the most common questions I encounter involves the relative attractiveness of investing in stocks versus investing in real estate. The short version is that it's somewhat akin to comparing vanilla and chocolate ice cream. They are different, and as your net worth grows, you may even find that both have a role to play in your overall portfolio. Your personality will also inform your decision, as some people are more temperamentally geared toward stock ownership or real estate ownership, respectively.

Risks of Real Estate Investing

A substantial percentage of real estate returns are generated due to the use of leverage. A real estate property is acquired with a percentage of equity, the remainder financed with debt. This results in higher returns on equity for the real estate investor; but if things go poorly, it can result in ruin far more quickly than a portfolio of fully-paid common stocks. (That's true even if the latter declined by 90% in a Great Depression scenario, as no one could force you to liquidate).

Some Final Thoughts on Real Estate Investing

Of course, this is only the beginning of your journey to understanding the topic, as we've barely scratched the surface. Real estate investing takes years of practice, experience, and exposure to truly appreciate, understand, and master.

Investing In Real Estate Investors

With the never-ending changes in our Real Estate Markets real estate professionals are starting to pay attention to the sound of new commission streams of income. Some realtors have either shied away or ran-away from such terms as "Cap Rate," & "Cash-on-Cash Returns." Terms that only the 'smart' and 'numbers-oriented people use to determine if a Real Estate purchase is a "Good Deal", or not. A majority of the realtor brethren attended real estate school because they are excited and passionate about the promise of selling real estate and making a fantastic living. That being said "Times are a Changing."

Even if you live in a Hot Market where residential real estate sells in 2-3 days there is an old approach to real estate that is growing faster by the day.....Residential Real Estate Investors.

This deft group of real estate investors is taking real estate and the real estate investment world into a new era! No longer accepting the crazy volatility of the Dow Jones and NASDAQ families. Unwilling to accept the investment practices of their fore-fathers these Investors throw caution to the wind for returns above the traditional 5-6% in their Roth or IRA accounts. These Investors are bold and oftentimes aggressive. Today's Real Estate Investors are all about the fast fix-n-flip, high appreciation, and rock solid monthly cash-flows. Cutting their teeth on investment in their own home-towns is only the beginning as the Serious Investors turn to points outside their own back-yards to other regions that demonstrate greater promise and higher returns. You may say well how does this older adult view their investment opportunities? For starters the age of these stealth hunters ranges from 28 to 68. " The young real estate entrepreneurs are making their dreams happen to the tune of 3-5 acquisitions a year! Got your attention now? The typical Investor has good to great credit scores. Excellent cash reserves or hidden resources of partners with cash, and a willingness to make the deal happen at nearly any cost. The best kept secret of all is that these investing beasts travel in packs. Where you see one another is very close behind. In other words they know the people that you need to know to grow your investor database even larger. If the real estate professional does a good job the happy clients are likely to refer many of their fellow-investors. Not just investor clients but their regular every-day real estate business. Face it, if you can demonstrate to your clients how adept you are with their largest personal purchase of real estate, then wouldn't you suppose they will be over their "trusted real estate advisors" opinion on buying a basic home, condo or beach house?

So what if you haven't been focused in the real estate investment sector. And you are thinking this all sounds pretty good, let's give it a try. First question to ask yourself is who have your clients been working with or exploring their options of real estate investing with over the past 3-4 months. Statistically 6 out of 10 clients have considered investing in real estate or have already begun doing so before their realtor even has a chance to blink an eye. Got your attention now?

1. Real Estate Investors are literally everywhere. Successfully tapping into your current database could increase your annual commissions by 20-30%.

2. Real Estate Investors will be loyal to the professional that helps fill the gap of their investment education. Workshops, mentoring groups, finding the "golden deals" in your market makes a huge impact!

3. Investing in Real Estate Investors doesn't have to mean that you lose your "typical" residential realtor position.

Being a real estate investment specialist means you are smarter than the average realtor in the market.

4. Mortgage professionals are struggling to provide real estate investors with property deals, so when you can place an investor into a good deal the referrals will begin to flow even more.

5. Real Estate Investors tend to be more conscientious about your personal time away. Investors also like to shop Monday-Friday for their deals before the "Weekend Warrior" investors get out into the competition. This translates into more normal hours and days of operation for you and your business.

6. Real Estate Investors buy-sell cycles are shorter than primary home purchasers resulting in more transactions in shorter time-frames.

RESIDENTIAL REAL ESTATE INVESTING - IS RESIDENTIAL REAL ESTATE INVESTING THE BEST WAY TO MAKE MONEY?

At over $20 trillion in size, the residential real estate market has a substantial influence on the U.S. economy. In fact, the single-family home market is several times larger than the entire commercial real estate industry.

But investors often ask whether residential real estate investing is better than investing in commercial real estate?

The answer is - it depends.

Each investor has a different skill set as well as vastly different financial resources. In addition, investors have varying backgrounds and interests. Money can be made with both. The investor needs to do what works best for them. Residential real estate investing may be the best choice for many, but not all investors.

There are many advocates of commercial real estate investing, but there are a couple of reasons that I generally favor residential real estate investing over commercial real estate.

First of all, an important factor that distinguishes residential real estate investing as compared to investing in commercial real estate is that the pricing of single-family homes is often driven by inefficient information. This means that pricing and market data is incorporated at a slower rate into the marketplace as compared to commercial real estate. This can enable the astute investor to better analyze price movements and allow for improved market forecasting.

Residential real estate investing is largely dominated by single-family residences that have fewer sophisticated buyers and sellers. With commercial properties, there are many more institutional investors with extensive market experience. Accordingly, locating a good deal may be much more difficult in commercial real estate as compared to residential real estate. Investing in commercial real estate is generally dominated by skilled professionals, who have more financial resources than the individual investor.

In addition, the demand for residential real estate continues to increase. This demand has been fueled by many factors, including population growth and baby boomers. The population is growing while available land remains relatively constant.

Making Money In Residential Real Estate

Many excited real estate investors think they can get rich by using a bank loan to purchase and upgrade local fixer-uppers. While investing in real estate may be better than investing in the stock market – because the existence of small, local real estate markets creates inefficiencies investors can exploit – you'll need a more advanced level of understanding to make money in residential real estate. To go from handyman to real estate tycoon, you must understand the market, as well as the three key ingredients of strong real estate gains.

Look for a Healthy National Market

While experienced and astute real estate investors may be able to make some money in a weak countrywide real estate environment, the odds are against them; the odds of success for newer investors in such a market are even worse. Rising interest rates can throw a lot of cold water on an otherwise hot real estate market, because those who have purchased real estate with adjustable rate mortgages have to pay more to keep it, and not everyone can afford it. This leads to reduced demand for real estate, and prices fall accordingly.

Thus, when starting to build your real estate portfolio, the ideal time is in a declining interest-rate environment. Generally speaking, not only will your loan be less expensive, but, barring a momentary credit crunch, demand is likely to be higher, which can be withstood with good capital management.

Another desirable trait is a healthy gross domestic product (GDP), since this figure really speaks to the overall health of the economic system that supports the real estate market. In healthy GDP times, such as growth of over 3% annually, it is rare to see significant real estate weaknesses.

Lastly, unemployment-rate data is often the leading indicator of market softness. If people see few prospects for income where they live, they move. In turn, this greatly reduces home price appreciation (HPA).

Choose a Specific Location

If you find flat to falling interest rates, decent GDP growth, and respectable unemployment rates in the national market, you can start looking for a desirable local market. Seek out an area with relatively strong appreciation potential, relative to other markets. Well-publicized unemployment data from Case-Shiller Home Price Index, Bureau of Labor Statistics, or other sources are excellent indicators of the top real estate markets' future health.

Local unemployment data are often highly indicative of the housing data. The smart investor seeks to invest in a city showing healthy unemployment trends and relatively strong HPA data. Hopefully, this is a city where you live, and therefore have a strong grasp of the vagaries of the local marketplace – and thus can easily manage the property. However, with sound management controls, it can be possible to invest successfully in other locations where quality management partners are available.

Find the Urban Sprawl Inflection Point

Once you have found the ideal city for your desired investment, look for the urban sprawl hotspot. If you see the city expanding, and can tolerate some risk, then invest in real estate on the perimeter. However, if the market looks ominous or vague, stick to the inner rings, so as to have a buffer against reverse urban sprawl.

Warning signs telling you to stay away from the perimeter include material unemployment changes and/or slowing economic growth in the local area. You could also look at the underlying business health of the major employers in the area. If it is weak, layoffs are likely coming, which could start to suppress real estate values due to marginal attrition of labor supply. If the business health of the area's major employers is strong, the opposite is true.

Real estate values can vary widely within a metropolitan area. For example, if the average HPA in a city is 5%, it may be 2% downtown, 6% in the first suburban ring, and 10% in the second suburban ring. The third ring would likely be farmland with modest HPA potential. Note the phenomenon here: your most volatile real estate appreciation will happen in the outer ring adjacent to the farmland, because this is the outer cusp of the city. This location leverage is exploitable by owning the edge in growth markets. Logically, in a down market, you would want to be at the core. This is where the least depreciation is likely to occur, since full housing markets make this the least likely place for the disruption of balance in supply and demand.

Understanding investing risk in different areas of the city is very similar to understanding how financial instruments generally behave. Think of the urban area of a city as investment-grade bonds, the first suburban ring as equities, and the outer ring as derivatives. Understanding where the urban sprawl inflection is occurring in a city can bolster returns on the upside, or protect investment on the downside.

For fun, let us peel the onion one layer further, to find the hottest areas. Suppose that you decide to invest in the perimeter, since you see economic growth and growing labor demand in the area. You could try to anticipate the location of stoplights. That is where future commercial properties, such as suburban strip malls, will be built; as residential real estate development fills in around these future strip malls, property values will likely jump significantly relative to average real estate returns.

The opportunity for above-average rates of return seems greater in the real estate realm than the financial instrument realm, since there are fewer eyes looking at nonhomogenous units. Knowing the local market also produces an investment advantage. A long-term or buy-and-hold strategy is better if you have ample capital and limited opportunities, while a short-term or flipping strategy would make more sense if you have limited capital and tremendous insight into the sweet spots. Regardless of your time frame, you should first look for a strong national market, then a region where publicized data shows decent HPA opportunity. Finally, play the urban sprawl perimeter if you believe the area is growing, or stay away from it if you see it as shrinking. Understanding these key points can help maximize the value of any real estate portfolio.

Making Money from Real Estate Investing

When it comes to making money in real estate investing, there are really only a handful of ways to do it. Though the concepts are simple to understand, don't be fooled into thinking they can be easily implemented and executed. Grab a notebook and pencil, because in the next ten minutes, I'll walk you through a brief overview to help you understand the basics of real estate and how treatment pay no Federal income tax on their corporate earnings as long as they follow a few rules, including a requirement to distribute 90% or more of profits to shareholders as dividends.

One downside of investing in REITs is that, unlike common stocks, the dividends paid out on them are not "qualified dividends", meaning the owner can't take advantage of the low tax rates available for most dividends. Instead, dividends from real estate investment trusts are taxed at the investor's personal rate. On the upside, the IRS has subsequently ruled that REIT dividends generated within a tax shelter such as a Rollover IRA are largely not subject to the unrelated business income tax so you might be able to hold them in a retirement account without much worry of tax complexity, unlike a master limited partnership.

(If you're interested in learning more about these unique securities, start by checking out Real Estate Investing Through REITs, which covers REIT liquidity, equity, how to use REITs to your real estate investing advantage, and much more.)

Investing in Real Estate Through Home Ownership

For all the real estate investing options available to investors, the average person is going to get his or her first real estate ownership experience the traditional way: By purchasing a home.

I've never viewed the acquisition of a home quite the same way most of society does. Instead, think of a into equity ownership if it isn't repaid. These are sometimes used in the development of hotel franchises.

There are sub-specialties of real estate investing including:

Leasing a space so you have little capital tied up in it, improving it, then sub-leasing that same space to others for much higher rates, creating incredible returns on capital. An example is a well-run flexible office business in a major city where smaller or mobile workers can buy office time or rent specific offices.

Acquiring tax-lien certificates. These are an esoteric area of real estate investing and not appropriate for hands-off or inexperienced investors but which -- under the right circumstances, at the right time, and with the right sort of person -- generate high returns to compensate for the headaches and risks involved.

Real Estate Investment Trusts (REITs)

On top of all of this, you can actually invest in real estate through something known as a real estate investment trust, or REIT. An investor can buy REITs through a brokerage account, Roth IRA, or another custody account of some sort. REITs are unique because the tax structure under which they are operated was created back during the Eisenhower administration to encourage smaller investors to invest in real estate projects they otherwise wouldn't be able to afford, such as building shopping centers or hotels. Corporations that have opted for REIT successful real estate investors work in order to maximize their earnings.

The Three Primary Ways to Make Money from Real Estate Investments

There are three primary ways investors make money from real estate:

An increase in the property value,

Rental income collected by leasing out the property to tenants, and

Profits generated from business activity that depends upon the real estate.

In a nutshell, that is it. Of course, there are always other ways to directly or indirectly profit from real estate, such as learning to specialize in more esoteric areas like tax lien certificates, but those three items accounts for a vast majority of the passive income, and ultimate fortunes, that have been made in the real estate industry. By learning how to take advantage of them for your own portfolio, you can add another asset class to your overall asset allocation, increasing both diversification and, if implemented prudently, reducing risk.

1. Making Money from an Increase In the Property Value of Your Real Estate Investments

First, it's important you understand that property values do not always increase. This can become painfully evident during periods like the late 1980s and early 1990s, and the 2007-2009 real estate collapse. In fact, in many cases, property values rarely beat inflation. For example, if you own a $500,000 piece of real estate and inflation is 3%, your property might sell for $515,000 ($500,000 x 1.03%) but you aren't any richer than you were last year. That is, you can still buy the same amount of milk, bread, cheese, oil, gasoline, and other commodities (true, cheese may be down this year and gasoline up, but your standard of living would remain roughly the same).

The reason? The $15,000 gain wasn't real. It was nominal.

This happens because the government has to create money when it spends more than it takes in through taxes. All else equal, over time, this results in each existing dollar losing value and becoming worth less than it was in the past.

One of the ways that the savviest real estate investors can make money in real estate is to take advantage of a situation that seems to crop up every few decades: When the rate of inflation is projected to exceed the current rate of long-term debt, you might find people willing to gamble by acquiring properties, borrowing money to finance the purchase, and then waiting for inflation to increase. That way, they can pay off the mortgages with dollars that are worth far less. This represents a transfer from savers to debtors.

You saw a lot of real estate investors making money this way in the 1970s and early 1980s as inflation began to spiral out of control before Paul Volker took a 2x4 to its back and brought it under control by drastically raising interest rates.

The trick is to buy when cyclically adjusted cap rates are attractive or when you think there is a specific reason that a particular piece of real estate will someday be worth more than the present cap rate alone indicates it should be. For example, talented real estate developers can look at the right project, at the right time, at the right price, and quite literally create the future rental income to support a valuation that might otherwise appear rich based on present conditions because they understand economics, market factors, and consumers.

2. Making Money from Rental Income Generated by Your Real Estate Investments

Making money from collecting rents is so simple that every six year old who has ever played a game of Monopoly understands on a visceral level how the basics work. If you own a house, apartment building, office building, hotel, or any other real estate investment, you can charge people rent in exchange for allowing them to use the property or facility. Of course, simple and easy are not the same thing. If you own apartment buildings or rental houses, you might find yourself dealing with everything from broken toilets to tenants who operated meth labs.

If you own strip malls or office buildings, you might have to deal with a business that leased from you going bankrupt. If you own industrial warehouses, you might find yourself facing environmental investigations for the actions of the tenants who used your property. If you own storage units, theft could be a concern. Real estate investments are not the type you can phone in and expect everything to go well.

The good news is that there are tools available that make comparisons between potential real estate investments easier. One of these, which will become invaluable to you on your quest to make money from real estate is a special financial ratio called the cap rate, which is short for "capitalization rate". If a property earns $100,000 per year and sells for $1,000,000, you would divide the earnings ($100,000) by the price tag ($1,000,000) and get 0.1, or 10%. That means the cap rate of the property is 10%, or that you would earn an expected 10% on your investment if you paid for the real estate entirely in cash and no debt.

Just as a stock is ultimately only worth the net present value of its discounted cash flows, a real estate is ultimate worth a combination of

1.) the utility it generates for its owner and

2.) the net present cash flows it generates relative to the price that was paid for the investment. Rental income can be a margin of safety that protects you during collapses. Certain types of real estate investments are better suited for this purpose. To go back to our earlier discussion of the challenges of making money from real estate, office buildings, to provide one illustration, typically involve long, multi-year leases.

Buy one at the right price, at the right time, and with the right tenant and lease maturity profile, and you could sail through a real estate collapse collecting above average rental checks that the companies leasing from you have to still provide (due to the lease agreement they signed) even when lower rates are available elsewhere. Get it wrong, though, and you could be locked in at sub par returns long after the market has recovered.

3. Making Money from Real Estate Business Operations

The final way of making money from real estate investments involves special services and business activities. If you own a hotel, you might sell on-demand movies to your guests. If you own an office building, you might make money from vending machines and parking garages. If you own a car wash, you might make money from time-controlled vacuum cleaners. These types of investments almost always require sub-specialty knowledge; e.g., there are men and women who spend their entire career specializing in designing, building, owning and operating car washes.

For those who rise to the top of their field and understand the intricacies of a particular market, the opportunity to make money can be endless.

FACTORS THAT INFLUENCE INVESTING IN RESIDENTIAL REAL ESTATE

Making money investing in residential real estate takes a lot of diligence and hard work. But fortunately it can be done and has been done by many.

However, successful investing in residential real estate rarely happens by accident and it rarely happens overnight. Those who are able to achieve their financial goals develop a plan and execute on that plan.

But the question still remains - How does the investor determine if it is the right time to begin investing in residential real estate?

There is no doubt that this can be a challenging task. There are many statistics available to the investor that will assist in the process. However, the investor needs to be aware of many of the factors that impact real estate valuation.

Economic factors that influence investing in residential real estate.

The investor should evaluate economic demand variables such as employment levels, wage rates, income levels and purchasing power, the availability of financing, interest rates, and transaction costs. The relationship of the local economy, the regional economy, and the national economy require scrutiny by the investor to properly identify the effects of all the variables on residential real estate prices.

Social factors that influence investing in residential real estate.

People have the basic desire for territory and companionship. Also, cost and prestige of certain locations motivate people to desire one location over another. The social factors of age distributions, education, crime rates, and pride of ownership, need consideration when analyzing residential real estate use patterns.

Legal, governmental, and political factors that influence investing in residential real estate

Local, regional, and national policies require evaluation to determine any effect on residential real estate prices in a given area. These policies affect the demand, and thus help drive sales prices. Policies on taxation, zoning, use controls, and rent controls can hasten real estate development or retard economic growth. The presence of amenities such as access, schools, public transportation, and fire and police protection influences demand and residential real estate valuations.

Physical, environmental, and locational factors that influence investing in residential real estate

Site and situation attributes enable the investor to analyze and determine patterns and trends in real estate values. Site attributes establish value by allowing the owner to use the inherent resources and features of the property. Common features for consideration in an analysis include size and land topography. Situation attributes establish value by virtue of proximity or accessibility to other resources such as the central business district, a shopping center, a school, a freeway, a waterfront, a sewage treatment plant, or a dump.

There are never any guarantees in real estate. But if astute investors carefully analyze the factors that influence investing in residential real estate, they will be one step ahead of the rest.

Checklist for Residential Real Estate Investing

However, moving from someone who owns simply owns real estate to someone who strategically invests and scales their portfolio requires a little more legwork—especially if you want to maximize your returns. There are also multiple investment strategies with real estate, and understanding your options will help narrow down the best approach for you.

But first things first. In this book, we'll run through a starting checklist for residential real estate investing, beginning with strategy, tips as you go through the process, and conventional advice you might want to think twice about.

Finding the strategy that works for you

There are plenty of residential real estate investing strategies, all varying in complexity.

Fix and Flip

The fix and flip business model is exactly how it sounds. This is where you find a property that you believe you can renovate and resell for a profit. This is usually a short-term investment strategy used by seasoned investors who can spot a good deal. Additionally, seasoned investors typically have connections and relationships with contractors they can call on right away to get renovations done within budget.

It's important to note that short-term real estate transactions are taxed differently than long-term investments (longer than a year).

Self-managed

The self-managed strategy is one where you as the property owner will also take on the management responsibilities. This approach is often considered by real estate investors who live close to their properties and have the bandwidth/moxie to handle things like maintenance, tenants screenings, paperwork and marketing the property, not to mention staying abreast of current landlord-tenant laws and regulations. This strategy restricts your purchasing footprint since you'll want to be within reasonable driving distance in case of emergencies or fix-it issues. On the flip side, you'll receive 100% of the rent while taking on a full landlord role.

Outsourced

There are myriad benefits to going with a professional property manager. They save you time, stress, and even money by avoiding problems that could lead to legal fees, vacancies, and damages related to mishandled repairs. Working with an experienced property manager who knows the local market and rental dynamics also frees you up to invest without geographic barriers, and own income properties in markets that meet your budget and investing goals. (Buying outside your primary market is also a great strategy from a diversification standpoint). Remote residential real estate investing is a growing trend and we're seeing more and more of it at Roofstock. In fact, the majority of our buyers live more than 1,000 miles away from their properties.

A helpful checklist for the real estate beginner

1. Get pre-approved

If you're serious about buying an investment property, it's helpful to get pre-approved for a mortgage. By doing this, you'll have an idea of what you can and cannot afford. Contact your local bank or mortgage officer to figure out what the top end of your price range is so you know where you stand. You can also take advantage of turnkey real estate marketplaces such as Roofstock, which provides trusted partners for all aspects of the investment process —including finance, insurance and property management.

It's also helpful to have a discussion with your lender about the type of loan that makes sense for you. For example, a 15-year mortgage may have lower rates and allow you to pay off your investment properties faster. With a 30-year loan, however, your money isn't as tied up. You may enjoy higher monthly cash flow and the added flexibility to use that income for an emergency fund or save it up for your next down payment on another investment property. It all depends on your budget and residential real estate investing criteria and knowing this upfront will help move things along. Be sure to consult your professional financial advisor about this.

Tip: When you purchase an investment property on Roofstock, you are free to use your own lender or one of our certified lenders. You can leverage Roofstock's resources and partners as little or as much as you want.

2. Set a few goals

These don't have to be set in stone and will likely evolve as you become more versed in the residential real estate investing space. But generally speaking, defining what's really important to you from the outset will make the decision process easier and also help you avoid analysis paralysis when narrowing down the sea of investment property options. Here is an example of some fundamental things to consider at the start of your investing journey:

Budget: Set a threshold that makes sense for you (and your wallet) and stick to it. If you're financing, you don't want to over-leverage yourself.

Risk/return tolerance: This is not absolute, but sometimes lower-yielding properties tend to be safer investments and higher-yielding homes come with a little more risk. Both potentially have a place in your rental portfolio—it's just a matter why you're investing in rental income properties and what you hope to achieve. Are you looking for higher monthly cash flow, more stability, or something in between?

Appreciation: This is the increase in the value of your investment property over time. If higher monthly cash flow isn't as critical and you care more about building up equity over time, you might focus on properties with higher appreciation potential. Knowing this will help you in narrowing down your options. For example, you might focus on relatively "newer" properties (for example - built after a certain year such as 1980), certain markets, neighborhood qualities, etc. and less on cap rate or monthly cash flow.

Cap rate: This is the estimated rate of return on an investment property. Cap rate is calculated by dividing net operating cash flow in the first year by the property purchase price. At Roofstock, our marketplace features a variety of cap rates generally ranging from 4-11%. As we touched on earlier, different cap rates (in theory) can signify varying levels of risk. Higher cap rates may correlate to a higher amount of risk in the purchase, and vice versa.

3. Learn some industry lingo

Like many first-time real estate investors, you've probably been browsing forums on Bigger Pockets, checking out articles from Landlordology, downloading Listen Money Matters podcasts, and spending some quality time with Investopedia (or not...we don't judge). What may seem like a lot of industry jargon and endless acronyms—1031s, REI, REITs, NOI, leverage, LTV, amortization, Cap Ex—will all become familiar territory in due time. By learning more about the language investors use—and not just what it is, but why it matters—you'll feel more confident and be in a better position to make informed decisions.

4. Be conservative when it comes to estimating your costs

From closing costs to unexpected vacancies to renovations and fixes, there's a good chance operating costs will be more than you initially expect. This doesn't mean you made a bad investment, it just means your expectations around potential operating expenses may have been underestimated from the outset. Some costs are easy to predict. These include basic operating expenses, closing costs and other assumptions outlined in your financial pro forma such as property taxes, management fees and insurance. Other expenses are impossible to foresee and simply come with the territory of owning rental property. We suggest maintaining a minimum contingency fund of about 1-2% of the purchase price.

5. The place you buy doesn't have to be in a place you'd live

Judging a property based on curb appeal alone is a common mistake new real estate investors frequently make. While it's natural to form an opinion based on personal bias, remember: You're not the one who's moving in. Instead, ask yourself: "Is the property I'm buying going to be desirable to some set of tenants? Whether it's a retiree, a group of college students, a family with kids in high school or someone who needs to live near the airport, different things are going to matter to different people. As an investor it's not about your personal preferences—it's about whether the property will drive the the kind of returns you're looking for. Don't pass up a property based on aesthetics alone as some of the most profitable rental homes don't look that special at first glance.

6. Focus on the area, not just the home itself

As an investor, location should be an important factor in your purchase decision. Is the city growing? Does it have a diversified economy? Did a major company recently re-locate there or open a second headquarters? What about the neighborhood? How are the schools and what kinds of nearby amenities are there? Do a little research on the market(s) you're considering (this can actually be kind of fun and exciting) to get an idea of what's happening in the area. You can even speak with a local property manager and get their take on the rental market dynamics. Tip: At Roofstock, we can connect you directly with one of our certified property managers who would be happy to give you some additional insight.

7. Partner up

The company you keep will define who you are as investor and help you get the most out of your investment properties. By leveraging the tools and data of today with the knowledge and services of traditional real estate professionals, the possibilities increase tenfold. From property managers and real estate agents, to handy apps and software, to innovative marketplaces that let you buy turnkey properties fully online, they all have value to provide.

A Return To The Fundamentals of Residential Real Estate Investing

When real estate is going up, up, up, investing in real estate can seem easy. All ships rise with a rising tide, and even if you've bought a deal with no equity and no cash flow, you can still make money if you're in the right place at the right time.

However, it's hard to time the market without a lot of research and market knowledge. A better strategy is to make sure you understand the four profit centers for residential real estate investing, and make sure your next residential real estate investment deal takes ALL of these into account.

Cash Flow - How much money does the residential income property bring in every month, after expenses are paid? This seems like it should be easy to calculate if you know how much the rental income is and how much the mortgage payment is. However, once you factor in everything else that goes into taking care of a rental property - things like vacancy, expenses, repairs and maintenance, advertising, bookkeeping, legal fees and the like, it begins to really add up.

Appreciation - Having the property go up in value while you own it has historically been the most profitable part about owning real estate. However, as we've seen recently, real estate can also go DOWN in value, too. Leverage (your bank loan in this case) is a double-edged sword. It can increase your rate of return if you buy in an appreciating area, but it can also increase your rate of loss when your property goes down in value. For a realistic, low-risk property investment, plan to hold your residential real estate investment property for at least 5 years. This should give you the ability to weather the ups and downs in the market so you can see at a time when it makes sense, from a profit standpoint.

Debt Pay down - Each month when you make that mortgage payment to the bank, a tiny portion of it is going to reduce the balance of your loan. Because of the way mortgages are structured, a normally amortizing loan has a very small amount of debt pay down at the beginning, but if you do manage to keep the loan in place for a number of years, you'll see that as you get closer to the end of the loan term, more and more of your principle is being used to retire the debt. Of course, all this assumes that you have an amortizing loan in the first place. If you have an interest-only loan, your payments will be lower, but you won't benefit from any loan pay down. I find that if you are planning to hold the property for 5-7 years or less, it makes sense to look at an interest-only loan, since the debt pay down you'd accrue during this time is minimal, and it can help your cash flow to have an interest-only loan, as long as interest rate adjustments upward don't increase your payments sooner than you were expecting and ruin your cash flow. If you plan to hold onto the property long term, and/or you have a great interest rate, it makes sense to get an accruing loan that will eventually reduce the balance of your investment loan and make it go away. Make sure you run the numbers on your real estate investing strategy to see if it makes sense for you to get a fixed rate loan or an interest only loan. In some cases, it may make sense to refinance your property to increase your cash flow or your rate of return, rather than selling it.

Tax Write-Offs - For the right person, tax write-offs can be a big benefit of real estate investing. But they're not the panacea that they're sometimes made out to be. Individuals who are hit with the AMT (Alternative

Minimum Tax), who have a lot of properties but are not real estate professionals, or who are not actively involved in their real estate investments may find that they are cut off from some of the sweetest tax breaks provided by the IRS.

HOW TO PREPARE YOURSELF TO MEET AND CAPTURE REAL ESTATE INVESTORS

The common mistake inexperienced real estate agents make when working with rental property is to incorrectly understand what real estate investors require from an agent in order to make investment decisions.

The fault stems from the fact that most agents do not fully grasp the notion that real estate investing - unlike residential transactions - concerns the issue of profitability. For unlike residential property where curb appeal, school zones and floor plans play a major role in the decision making, this is not the case with rental income property.

Real estate investing is a money business to investors. Amenities are not ignored, but are routinely considered only by what impact they would have on the cash flow and rate of return. What someone interested in buying or selling rental property really wants to know is "How much money will I make?"

Unfortunately for most agents, however, this is where the dialogue becomes murky because the agent has no credible way to respond. And as a result, the all-important first encounter so vitally necessary for the agent to impress the investor is tainted by inexperience - therein reducing the agent's chance to capture the investor's loyalty and any future hope of a transaction to probably zero.

I've witnessed it dozens of times during my thirty-year experience working with rental property investors. When you blow the first encounter with an investor (who is neither a family member nor close friend) you should expect the words you will hear from the investor on any subsequent contact will be "Thank you, but I'm working with someone else."

It's a familiar theme. Investor contacts agent regarding a rental property, then after several minutes realizes that he or she understands little-to-nothing about income property investing and moves on.

I've certainly been there - hey, you've probably been there. It's the nature of what residential realtors experience when they are not adequately prepared to meet and capture investors during an initial encounter.

Okay, so how do you prepare?

Make an investment in a real estate investment software solution. As you use it you will become acquainted with the financial data investors are looking for as well as the types of returns. More importantly, though, you will be amply prepared to create cash flow and rates of return analysis presentations for rental income property on-the-spot.

Think about it.

The next time a potential buyer asks you about some particular income property currently for sale you don't have to present what the listing agent prepared (which is not a good idea) and instead you can present your own reports personalized with your name and contact information.

The same holds true for potential sellers. An investment software solution will enable you create reports that help support your suggested asking price. Moreover, they convey the awareness that you are engaged in investing and prepared to sell rental property (which in turn instills investor confidence and results in loyalty).

Software is not a magic bullet - you still have to apply some charm when you make the presentations.

But real estate investment software does equip you with the best tool possible to adequately service rental properties and investors. You instantly take a qualifying position ahead of other residential agents, and more importantly, you significantly improve your chances to produce rental property transactions having a ready answer for investors who ask, "How much money will I make?"

CHAPTER TWO

STARTING A BUSINESS IN RESIDENTIAL REAL ESTATE INVESTING

Opting to invest in residential real estate has become a popular trend amongst many investors. It is in human nature for investors to invest when the market is rising in terms of stock, gold, and housing and automatically stop investing when the market falls. In true essence this leads to many investors leaving a lot of money that could easily be earned.

If you take the time to understand the fundamental principals that come with real estate investment, you will be able to capitalize on various aspects that many other investors are known to miss out on.

The thing you have to understand is that real estate investing is no quick get rich scheme. Yes it does offer you the opportunity to make some quick cash through flipping houses however the word investment should always be related to long term. This will ensure you are more successful.

While most of the investors will be packing their bags to go home when the market falls, this is where you can utilise on the fundamental principals that you have learnt and capitalize in terms of large profits. You will be able to make money regardless of the market status.

The fundamentals

When the market for real estate is rising in terms of equity, it makes it very easy for any "layman" off the street to even make money in the real estate business. What you have to make sure is that you put your money at the right place at the right time.

No matter how much research you do, being able to predict the market will be impossible. For this reason it is better if you simply opt to understand four various profit centres.

1.Cash Flow - This simply entails of the amount of money your residential income property brings in. Even though it may seen quite simple to calculate, many tend to over look various factors. You need to include all the expenses that are needed to be paid. These would include mortgage payments, repairs, advertising, debts, maintenance etc. It is important you keep a tally of all expenses to give you a fair value of cash flow.

2. Appreciation - It is possible for the market value of your house to increase while you own it. This is seen to be one of the fastest ways to earn really good money. However seeing that the market is quite volatile, you never know what to expect. For this reason it is highly recommended that you keep your residential property for at least a five year period before you decide to sell it off once again.

3. Debt pay down - Now when you own a residential property you would be expected to make monthly mortgage payments. These simply are accumulated over time to reduce the amount of loan that you own to the lending company. Now seeing that we are aiming to look at long term investments there are a few things that you need to keep in mind. Now the common loan system that everyone opts for will simply include a monthly repayment with interest. If you are planning to hold your property for a couple of years, you will see that you are actually paying more than you initially took out because of the interest rate. Seeing that you are going to be looking to sell of your property in the future it is ideal to go for an interest based loan only. This will result to me more profitable for you in the long run.

4. Tax write offs - It is quite common for one to have to pay Alternative Minimum Tax on various real estate properties depending on weather or not you match the criteria. The tax is usually based on the earned income and you may even see your self having to pay short term capital gains tax as well. However there is a possibility that you can have your tax written off which can prove to be quite beneficial for many. The problem with those investors that deal with houses on a flipping houses basis, there income is treated as earned income. This means you would have to pay the full amount of tax that you would do for a 9 to 5 job as well.

If you stick to the strategies and fundamentals that have been highlighted above, you are known to be able to earn a good amount of money regardless of the market change. Any market trend that moves in your favour will obviously boost your profit prospects but even if the market moves in a negative favour, you are still going to be able to "fight" your way through.

9 WAYS TO INVEST IN REAL ESTATE WITHOUT BUYING PROPERTY

Last year's housing market was one for the record books, with the gains partly driven by tightening inventories and exceedingly low mortgage rates. In some pockets of the country, housing prices rose well over 10 percent on average.

But, it's not only the big coastal cities that are seeing huge growth. A recent survey from GoBankingRates revealed that many cities with the most growth were inland, including: Buffalo, New York (34.6%), Atlanta, Georgia (24.54%), and Cincinnati, Ohio (20.6%).

With this in mind, you may be wondering if you should throw your hat in the ring and invest in real estate — or, if you're too late. You may also be wondering if you should invest in real estate in a traditional sense — as in, becoming a landlord.

Now, here's the good news. Not only is now still a good time to invest in real estate since more growth is likely on its way, but there are also more ways than ever to invest in housing without dealing with tenants or the other minutiae of landlord work.

1: Invest in real estate ETFs

An exchange-traded fund, also known as an ETF, is a collection of stocks or bonds in a single fund. ETFs are similar to index funds and mutual funds in the fact they come with the same broad diversification and low costs over all.

If you're angling to invest in real estate but also want to diversify, investing in a real-estate themed ETF can be a smart move. Vanguard's VNQ, for example, is a real estate ETF that invests in stocks issued by real estate investment trusts (REITs) that purchase office buildings, hotels, and other types of property. IYR is another real estate ETF that works similarly since it offers targeted access to domestic real estate stocks and REITs.

There are plenty of other ETFs that offer exposure to real estate, too, so make sure to do your research and consider the possibilities.

2: Invest in real estate mutual funds

Just like you can invest in real estate ETFs, you can also invest in real estate mutual funds.

TIREX is another real estate mutual fund to consider with $1.9 billion in assets, broad diversification among real estate holdings, and low fees.

3: Invest in REITs

Consumers invest in REITs for the same reason they invest in real estate ETFs and mutual funds; they want to invest in real estate without holding physical property. REITs let you do exactly that while also diversifying your holdings based on the type of real estate class each REIT invests in.

With that being said, I typically suggest clients stay away from non-traded REITs and buy only publicly-traded REITs instead. The U.S. Securities and Exchange Commission (SEC) recently came out to warn against non-traded REITs, noting their lack of liquidity, high fees, and lack of value transparency create undue risk.

4: Invest in a real estate focused company.

There are many companies that own and manage real estate without operating as a REIT. The difference is, you'll have to dig to find them and they may pay a lower dividend than a REIT.

Companies that are real estate-focused can include hotels, resort operators, timeshare companies, and commercial real estate developers, for example. Make sure to conduct due diligence before you buy stock in individual companies, but this option can be a good one if you want exposure to a specific type of real estate investment and have time to research historical data, company history, and other details.

5: Invest in home construction

If you look at real estate market growth over the last decade or longer, it's easy to see that much of it is the result of limited housing inventory. For this reason, many predict that construction of new homes will continue to boom over the next few decades or more.

In that sense, it's easy to see why investing in the construction side of the industry could also be smart. An entire industry of homebuilders will need to develop new neighborhoods and rehabilitate old ones, after all, so now may be a good time to buy in.

Large homebuilders to watch include LGI Homes (LGIH), Lennar (LEN), D.R. Horton (DHI), and Pulte Homes (PHM), but there are plenty of others to discover on your own.

6: Hire a property manager

While you don't have to buy physical property to invest in real estate, there's at least one strategy that can help you have your cake and eat it, too. Many investors who want exposure to rental real estate they can see and touch go ahead and buy rentals but then hire a property manager to do all the heavy lifting.

The key to making sure this strategy works is ensuring you only invest in properties with enough cash flow to pay for a property manager and still score a sizeable rate of return.

7: Invest in real estate notes

Real estate notes are a type of investment you can buy if you're interested in investing in real estate but don't necessarily want to deal with a brick-and-mortar building. When you're investing in real estate notes through a bank, you're typically buying debt at prices that are well below what a retail investor would pay.

8: Hard money loans

If you don't like any of the other ideas on this list but have cash to lend, you can also consider giving a hard money loan.

Either way, hard money loans directly to real estate investors are another strategy to consider if you want to invest in real estate but don't want to deal with a property and the headaches that come with it.

9: Invest in real estate online

Last but not least, don't forget about all the new companies that have cropped up to help investors get involved in real estate without getting their hands dirty.

Investing with either company is similar to investing in REITs in that your money is pooled with cash from other investors who take advantage of the platform. The cash you invest may be used to purchase residential property, commercial real estate, apartment buildings, and more. Ultimately, you get the benefit of dividends and distributions and long-term appreciation of the properties you "own."

How to Invest: 4 Options for Real Estate Investing.

Typically, real estate investing is done in four ways: purchasing fix-and-flips, buy-and-hold investing, purchasing commercial real estate, and buying vacation rental property. Buy and hold investing is the most common type of real estate investment and can usually be done for a 10 percent to 20 percent down payment plus two percent to five percent in closing costs.

Types of Real Estate Investing & Who They're Best For

Here are four ways to get involved with real estate investing:

1. Fix & Flip Real Estate Investing

Fix-and-flip real estate investing is for short-term investors wanting to purchase, renovate, and sell a house, typically within 12 months. Fix-and-flippers look for rehab projects in poor condition that if renovated, can sell for a comparatively high return.

Who Fix & Flips Are Right For

Real estate professionals such as realtors, brokers, and contractors, as well as experienced rehabbers, are most suited for a fix-and-flip project. This is because rehabs are often funded by hard money loans with unique terms and typically require extensive renovations.

As a rule of thumb, fix-and-flip real estate investing is best for investors with two to three-plus past rehab projects. However, fix-and-flippers are sometimes inexperienced rehabbers who instead rely on licensed contractors to help them with renovations. When this is the case, the contractor provides the scope of the rehab work as well as a bid for the expected overall cost.

Fixing-and-flipping properties is the right real estate investment strategy for the following:

Timeline: Three-plus months to devote to a fix-and-flip project, which gives you time to purchase, renovation, and sell.

Funds: $30,000 in cash or credit to cover hard money rehab loan. Average fix-and-flip properties sell for $150,000, and hard money lenders typically require fix-and-flippers to cover 20 percent of a property's expected sale price after renovations, known as After Repair Value (ARV).

For more information on investing in real estate through fix-and-flips, read our ultimate guide on how to make money flipping houses.

Fix & Flip Costs

Holding costs for fix-and-flip real estate investments generally include:

Mortgage Payments: Interest only payments with rates typically between 7% and 12%

Property Taxes: Generally around 2% of property's appraised value

Utilities: Typically $100 to $200 per month, depending on property size and usage

HOA Fees: If the property is in an HOA or condominium association, these fees vary based on unit size and amenities.

Fix-and-flip investors can also extend the loan beyond the term for additional penalties and fees. This might happen if an inexperienced fix-and-flipper hits unseen issues that extend the rehab timeline. This situation also might occur if a fix-and-flip investor can't sell the property for the price they expected and hold onto it for longer. Of course, this adds to your holding costs and further eats into your profits.

Funding for Fix & Flip Real Estate Investments.

Fix-and-flip real estate investing is typically financed using a hard money loan. These are short-term interest only loans that lump the purchase price and rehab budget together as a single loan. Unlike conventional mortgages, rehab loans can be used to finance a house in poor condition and are therefore the most popular loan option for fix-and-flippers.

Hard money lenders like LendingHome charge interest rates and fees between:

Interest Rates: 7.5% – 12%

Lender Fees: 1.5% – 2.5%, which are taken directly out of the loan.

Hard money loans are the most common type of fix-and-flip financing, but some investors make real estate investments using all cash. Cash allows investors to purchase houses quicker as compared to rehab loans and also result in lower holding fees, thus increasing an investor's potential profit.

Costs that eat into your potential profit include such things as:

   Lender Fees: Between 1.5% and 5 % of the loan

   Closing Costs: 2% – 5% of purchase price

   Rehab Budget: Dependent on scope of work

   Utilities: Typically around $100 to $200 per month

    Property Taxes: Roughly equal to 2% of the property value

Average Return of a Fix & Flip

The average return on a successful real estate flip is a 20 percent gross return, calculated by taking the average gross profit of $30,000 and dividing it by the average sale price of $150,000. The average net profit on a fix-and-flip is generally a 15 percent return. This means that if you do it right, you should only incur total costs equal to 5 percent of the property's sale price including holding costs.

Profit from real estate investing comes exclusively from the sale of the property. The net return is typically considered a short-term capital gain and requires investors to pay taxes at their ordinary tax rate. For more information on real estate tax deductions and benefits, check out our ultimate guide on real estate tax deductions and our free worksheet.

Potential Risks of Fix & Flips

While the reward is high, there are many potential risks when it comes to fix-and-flip real estate investing. This is especially true for real estate investing for beginners, who aren't used to managing rehab budgets and timelines.

Specifically, fix-and-flip investors are exposed to:

- Higher than expected rehab costs
- Higher than expected holding costs
- Loan extension penalties

The longer it takes to renovate and sell a fixer-upper, the longer the overall timeline and the higher the potential holding costs will be. If this is the case, you also might be at risk for loan extension fees with your hard money lender as you work on an extended timeline. Further, many fix-and-flip projects naturally result in higher than expected rehab costs that increase your out-of-pocket expenses.

Average Investment Timeline for a Fix & Flip

The average timeline for one fix-and-flip project is six months, and the term of a rehab loan offered by a hard money lender like LendingHome is typically around 12 months. However, the faster a rehab investor can sell a fixer-upper, the fewer holding costs a flipper incurs, thus increasing potential profit. Holding costs are the monthly costs that rehab investors have to cover until they can sell the property.

Where to Get Fix and Flip Loans

You can get fix-and-flip loans through online hard money lenders and local hard money lenders. LendingHome is an online nationwide lender that offers fix-and-flip loans for investors. They can get you preapproved online in just a few minutes and they offer competitive rates.

2. Buy-and-Hold Residential Real Estate Investing

Buy-and-hold investors are long-term investors who purchase one or more rental properties. These properties include single family homes, apartment buildings, and multifamily buildings. They make money off of monthly rental income as well as real estate investment appreciation. Some buy-and-hold investors also start as rehabbers, relying on rehab loans to renovate a property before renting it out and refinancing to a conventional mortgage.

Who Buy & Hold Real Estate Investing Is Right For

Buy-and-hold investing is suitable for passive long-term investors looking to purchase residential real estate and hold it long-term. It's right for portfolio investors with multiple properties, as well as landlords who manage their own properties. Buy-and-hold investing is also right for investors who own duplexes and multifamily properties.

Specifically, buy-and-hold real estate investing is good for:

Portfolio Investors: Typically own four to ten-plus rental properties and rely on property management companies

Landlords: Typically own one to three rental properties and manage the properties themselves

Turnkey Properties: Investor who purchase properties away from their home and purchased them with a tenant and management company in place

1031 Exchanges: Investors who want to engage in a like-kind exchange by selling one real estate investment and purchasing another for tax benefits.

Buy and Hold Real Estate Investing Costs

Typical costs associated with a buy-and-hold real estate investment include:

Financing Costs: Loan origination fees and any points

Closing Costs: Generally 2% to 5% of the purchase price

Maintenance Costs: Costs to upkeep the property

Utilities: For common areas that the landlord is responsible for paying.

Property Taxes: Roughly equal to 2% of the property's purchase price.

Rental Property Insurance: Yearly average $1,473 to $1,596 on a $200,000 investment property.

HOA Fees: If the property is a condo or part of an HOA, fees cover things like exterior maintenance, common area utilities, and amenities.

Funding for Buy & Hold Real Estate Investing

Buy-and-hold investors, both portfolio investors and landlords, typically rely on conventional mortgages to fund their investment purchases.

The typical terms of a conventional investment property loan are as follows:

Loan Amount: 80% – 96.5% of a house's purchase price

Interest Rates: 4.5% – 6.5%

Lender Fees: 0% – 1%

Terms: 15 years – 30 years

Average Return on Buy & Hold Real Estate Investments

The average return on a buy-and-hold property sale price is generally around 9 percent ROI. A buy-and-hold investor's annual ROI is inclusive of both annual rental income plus any price appreciation earned through the eventual sale.

ROI is also net of any costs, which include such things as:

Mortgage Payments: Based on the purchase price and amortized over 15 to 30 years.

Property Taxes: Roughly 2% of fair market value annually.

Repairs and Maintenance for Landlords: Roughly 2% of fair market value annually.

Property management Fees for Portfolio Investors: Typically 15% to 35% of annual gross rental income.

Further, an investor can increase his or her returns if REO properties or foreclosures are purchased. This is because the sales prices are generally less.

Potential Risks of Buy & Hold Real Estate Investing

Portfolio investors and landlords face the same buy-and-hold risks with their rental properties. The main risks of buy-and-hold real estate investing is the occupancy rate and the potential for price depreciation. You can overcome low occupancy rates by pricing your rental units correctly. Price depreciation may be unavoidable at times, but by researching the neighborhood and buying in stable or up-and-coming areas, you can help prevent it.

Specifically, buy-and-hold investors are at risk of:

Occupancy Risk: Rental property won't be filled by tenants full-time, which eats into the annual ROI. It also describes tenants leaving a rental property in poor condition, which requires the owner to spend more on repairs and maintenance.

Price Depreciation: The real estate market can dip lower than the total cost of the borrower's mortgage, causing an investor to become "underwater." This happens when an investor owes more on a property than it's currently worth.

Personal Default: Monthly amortized mortgage payments sometimes become too much of a burden, and buy-and-hold investors might become delinquent on their mortgage payments. This can result in bankruptcy and/or foreclosure, both of which hurt your personal credit. This risk is highest when landlords borrow up to 50 percent of their annual income or when portfolio investors invest in too many properties at once.

Liability Risk: Landlords and portfolio investors can be found liable for on-site injuries due to negligence or lack of care. Buy-and-hold investors can protect themselves with landlord liability insurance.

Average Investment Timeline for Buy & Hold Properties

Buy-and-hold investors typically hold a house for five to 30-plus years. However, as long as portfolio investors and landlords are able to keep long-term tenants, the trend is to hold onto the investment property for as long as 30 years or more. The benefit is that it builds family wealth through equity and property appreciation.

However, long-term buy-and-hold investors often rely on the real estate market to dictate their investment timelines. If the value of the property is growing, investors are more likely to hold. If the market peaks, buy-and-hold investors are more likely to sell their properties and realize their actual gains.

Where to Get Buy and Hold Investment Loans

For more information on rehab loans for buy-and-hold investors, check out Visio Lending. Rates are competitive for prime borrowers, and prequalification can be done online in just a few minutes. Funding usually takes 21 business days.

3. Commercial Real Estate Investing

Commercial real estate investing is investing in property that is used for commercial and not residential purposes. The sole purpose of the property is for conducting business. Commercial properties are purchased by investors and leased out to companies, and include such things as office spaces, restaurants, and retail stores. Commercial real estate investors, therefore, are long-term investors who earn monthly lease income and price appreciation.

Who Commercial Real Estate Investing Is Right For

Commercial real estate investing is generally right for business owners who want to own the property their business is located in. It's also right for experienced investors because it can be more complicated and more expensive than investing in residential real estate. It can be right for real estate beginners who have an experienced partner or mentor. Commercial real estate investors are usually people or entities who are flush with cash or willing to take out large loans and become highly levered.

The most common types of commercial real estate investors include:

Businesses and corporations seeking their own office spaces.

Real estate investment funds that invest in commercial-only or commercial+residential.

Limited partnerships that pool funds and diversify risk for smaller commercial investors.

Experienced individual investors with a higher tolerance for risk, access to funding, and familiarity with commercial real estate.

Each of these investors seeks to purchase and lease a property long term. This is aided by the fact that commercial mortgage terms can span up to 25 years, and average leases range from three to five years, making it a good buy-and-hold opportunity. Large commercial property management companies help these commercial buy-and-hold investors by managing their investments.

CBRE and Jones Lang LaSalle (JLL), for example, are two of the largest commercial real estate companies and help facilitate sales, retain tenants, negotiate leases and more. These companies, of course, charge for their services, which can eat into a commercial real estate investor's profits.

Commercial Real Estate Costs

Commercial real estate investment costs generally include:

Lender Fees: Loan origination fees and any points the lender charges

Closing Costs: Generally 2% – 5 % of the purchase price

Property Taxes: Generally higher than residential real estate investments, and they can vary widely based on location and building size

Licenses: Any specific licenses needed to operate the business

Utilities: Landlord may pay for common areas, and the tenant generally pays all other utilities.

Some commercial real estate costs such as property taxes, maintenance and licenses are generally paid in part or in full by the tenant as part of the terms of their lease.

Funding for a Commercial Real Estate Investment

Commercial real estate properties are typically purchased using commercial real estate loans. Commercial mortgages are funded by traditional banks and have loan terms between five years and 25 years, with the exception of commercial hard money loans. The typical interest rates found on a commercial loan can be fixed or variable, and are typically between 4.5 percent and 6.75 percent. This means that some commercial mortgages will have a balloon payment towards the end of the loan.

These commercial loans come in four different types:

Traditional commercial mortgage

SBA 7(a) loan for commercial real estate

CDC/SBA 504 loan for commercial real estate

Hard money loans for commercial real estate

Commercial mortgages will usually have lender fees known as "points."

Commercial real estate investors sometimes rely on hard money loans to fund their investment purchases. This is typically the case when a commercial real estate investor wants to renovate a property, either to sell or to lease out long term. Commercial investors might also need to move fast and commercial mortgage approval will take too long. When this happens, investors refinance to a commercial mortgage at a later date.

Hard money loans for commercial ventures have the same terms, such as interest rates between seven percent and 12 percent, lender fees between 1.5 percent and 2.5 percent, and term length between one year and 3 years.

Average Return on Commercial Real Estate Investing.

The 20-year average return on commercial real estate shows that the annual return is currently at a 9.5 percent gross return on investment (ROI). Commercial real estate investors earn a return on monthly lease income as well as on price appreciation when they sell their properties. Further, investors can increase their returns if they find a commercial real estate foreclosure or if they buy a property at auction.

However, the return is gross and therefore doesn't include any costs, such as:

Monthly Loan Payments: Based on the purchase price specific lender.

Commercial Property Taxes: Roughly 2% of fair market value annually.

Repairs and Maintenance for Investor Managed Properties: Generally 2% of fair market value annually.

Property Management Fees for Commercial Portfolio Investors: Generally 15% – 35% of annual gross lease income.

These expenses, similar to buy-and-hold residential investors, eat into the profits of a commercial real estate investor.

Potential Risks of Commercial Real Estate Investing

Commercial real estate investors generally face the following risks:

Occupancy Risk: Risk of an empty property and the risk of tenants destroying the property (which takes time and money to repair), and which negatively affects the ROI

Price Depreciation: The commercial real estate market can dip lower than the total cost of the borrower's commercial mortgage or hard money loan, causing a commercial investor to become "underwater." This happens when a commercial investor owes more on a commercial property than it's currently worth.

Personal Default: Commercial properties are large and carry a hefty price tag. Monthly amortized commercial loan payments sometimes become too much of a burden, and commercial investors might become delinquent on their loan payments.

Liability Risk: Owners of commercial real estate investors can be found liable for on-site injuries due to negligence or lack of care. Commercial investors can protect themselves with commercial real estate liability insurance.

Average Investment Timeline for Commercial Real Estate Investing

The average investment timeline of a commercial real estate investment is long term. This is because the financing terms are typically between five years and 25 years, and many investors hold commercial real estate properties longer than the maximum financing term.

The average lease for a commercial real estate property is also between three years and five years. Commercial real estate investors, therefore, have longer-term tenants than the tenants of residential properties. This extends an investor's average investment timeline and makes commercial investors more likely to buy-and-hold.

Where to Get Commercial Real Estate Loans

You can find a commercial real estate loan at your bank, credit union, or through an online lender like Patch of Land. Patch of Land lends on commercial properties such as apartment buildings, mixed-use buildings, and office and retail buildings. They can usually get you funded in as little as ten business days.

4. Investing in a Vacation Rental Property

Vacation rental property is a property that an investor buys to use as a vacation home and to rent out so they can offset the costs of home ownership and vacation-related costs. It's typically purchased in an area that has tourist attractions and amenities. It's a great way to get started in real estate investing for beginners because you get the benefit of using the property yourself and renting it when you're not using it. Typically, you hire a management company to manage the property while you're not there so it eases you into investing in real estate.

Who Vacation Rental Property Is Right for

A vacation rental property is generally right for the following:

A source of supplemental income

Rental property tax deductions

Real estate investing for beginners because it's easier than buying another type of real estate investment like an apartment building

You can enjoy your vacation rental property when you want

Rental income that offsets home ownership and vacation expenses

People generally purchase a vacation rental property for two primary reasons. First, they want to use the property as a second home with their friends and family. Secondly, it's purchased as a real estate investment that is rented during the periods they aren't using it.

Costs of a Vacation Rental Property

Typical costs of investing in a vacation rental property include:

Lender Fees: Loan origination fees and any lender points

Closing Costs: Generally 2% – 5% of the purchase price

Property Taxes: Varies depending on the size and location of the property

Vacation Rental Property Insurance: The average vacation rental insurance yearly premium is $2,000 – $3,000

Maintenance & Cleaning: Varies but averages 1% and 2% of the property's purchase price per year

Property Management Fees: Typically 15% – 30%-plus of the rent.

Keep in mind that a vacation rental property typically generates higher rents than a buy-and-hold real estate investment, but the costs such as insurance, cleaning, and maintenance are generally higher too.

Funding for a Vacation Rental Property

Investors typically fund a vacation rental property with a conforming loan, a portfolio loan, a multifamily loan or, in some cases, a short-term loan such as a hard money loan or a bridge loan. Some investors use all cash to buy a vacation rental property, but using financing is more common.

Conforming Loan for a Vacation Rental Property

A conforming loan used for a vacation rental home generally has more lenient qualifications than if used for a rental property. Lenders realize that borrowers will live there for part of the year, so they're not entirely dependent on rental income, which reduces the lender's risk. Qualifications vary by lender, but generally a 20 percent down payment is needed and a credit score over 680 (check your score free here).

Portfolio Loan for a Vacation Rental Property

An investor may use a portfolio loan to finance multiple properties at once or if they don't meet the criteria for a conforming loan. Portfolio loans usually offer lower personal qualifications and fewer property requirements than conforming loans.

For more information on portfolio loans, check out our in-depth guide to portfolio loans.

Multifamily Loan for Vacation Rental Property

An investor will generally use a multifamily loan to finance a vacation rental property with two to four units. There are four types of multifamily loans: conventional mortgages, government-backed loans, portfolio loans, and short-term multifamily financing. Each type of loan has its own lending criteria.

For more specific information on multifamily loans, check out our in-depth multifamily loan guide, which includes things like where to find multifamily loans and how to apply for them.

Average Returns on Investing in a Vacation Rental Property

Returns on a real estate investment such as a vacation rental property vary based on the purchase price of the property, the location, operating expenses and the occupancy rate. Typical returns on a vacation rental property are similar to a buy-and-hold investment and are usually around 9 percent to 12 percent.

Factors that affect your vacation property ROI are:

Management Fees: Average 28% for a vacation management company

Property Taxes: Typically 2%-plus of the assessed property value.

Financing Costs: Interest rate, lender fees and monthly mortgage payments.

Operational Expenses: Cleaning costs, maintenance, etc.

HOA Fees: If applicable, these can vary based on unit size and amenities in the building.

Occupancy Rates: The more the property is rented, the higher your ROI will be.

Potential Risks of Investing in a Vacation Rental Property.

There are always risks associated with real estate investing, and buying a vacation rental property is no different. Generally, the major risk will be a vacant property in between tenancies and being able to afford the carrying costs associated with the property.

Some risks of investing in a vacation rental property include:

Inconsistent cash flow because renters are usually seasonal.

You will have to cover carrying costs such as property taxes, maintenance, and utility bills, regardless of whether the property is rented or not.

You may have to pay a property manager to take care of operations.

Vacation rental properties are usually hit harder during economic downturns because people often eliminate or cut back on vacations to save money.

Average Timeline for Investing in Vacation Rental Property.

Investing in vacation rental property has a very similar timeline to investing in a primary residence or a multifamily property. Generally, the buyer decides on an area that is a popular vacation destination and works with a realtor who specializes in that area. This may take a few weeks to a few months, depending on the available inventory, your budget and your housing preferences.

After you find a vacation rental property, it usually takes 30 to 45 days to close on the property, if you're financing it. During this period, you will go through underwriting with a lender if you are financing the property. A title company will conduct a title search on the property and an appraisal will be ordered by your lender. You will also hire a property inspector.

Once all of this is done, the lender will give you a "clear to close" and the settlement will be scheduled for a convenient day for all parties. The settlement usually takes place within one to two weeks of the lender's final approval and is normally held at the title company's office. The actual settlement takes about 90 minutes.

For more information on buying vacation rental property, check out our in-depth guide on how to buy a vacation rental property, which includes things like what to look for in a vacation rental property and what areas to buy in.

Where to Get a Vacation Rental Property Loan

Finding the right lender for your vacation rental property doesn't have to be a headache. Fill out a short form on LendingTree and let lenders compete for your business. Their online marketplace lets you quickly compare rates, offers, and find a good fit. See your options online in minutes.

Alternative Real Estate Investing Options

There are several alternative ways of investing in real estate. These generally include real estate crowdfunding, investing in REITs, and tax liens. Each of these alternative investments has their own risks and rewards and are generally right for different kinds of investors.

Real estate crowdfunding companies provide opportunities to invest in loan-backed, single family homes, apartments, condos, and multi-unit properties. REITs are corporations that own or finance income-producing real estate. They typically own a portfolio of real estate within a specific sector and generally pay out 90 percent of annual profits to investors. Tax lien investing happens when an investor purchases a property after the owner has delinquent property taxes. Investors then earn interest and penalty payments.

Who Alternative Real Estate Investing Is Right For

Investing in alternative real estate investments may be right for people who don't want to be hands-on landlords. They can be right for passive short-term and long-term investors who want to get involved in real estate without purchasing a property outright.

The most popular alternative real estate investments are:

Real Estate Crowdfunding

Real estate crowdfunding pools money from multiple investors to fund a project or portfolio of projects. Real estate crowdfunding is right for passive accredited and non-accredited investors who want to invest in a project that would otherwise be out of their price range or geographic location.

The idea behind real estate crowdfunding websites is that they use a pool of accredited investors to fund the loans of various borrowers. This means that real estate crowdfunding investors invest in loans using their own cash.

Most real estate crowdfunding websites boast an average return of around 10 percent for both short-term and long-term opportunities. LendingHome, for example, lists average returns for accredited crowdfunding investors between 8 percent and 10 percent of net profit. Returns on a crowdfunding investment come as a portion of the interest rate charged to the borrower.

Since real estate crowdfunding investments are typically made on a loan-by-loan basis, there is always the risk of borrower default. When this happens, the borrower stops making their monthly payments and might not be able to repay the loan in full.

Investing in real estate crowdfunding can be done in about one month, which allows for due diligence and contracts to be executed. The real estate crowdfunding timeline is generally for the duration of the loan the developer took out, which is typically one to five years.

For more detailed information on real estate crowdfunding, read our in-depth real estate crowdfunding guide.

Real Estate Investment Trust (REITs) Investments

REITs are corporations that own or finance income-producing properties. They give investors more liquidity and can be traded like a stock without the investor acting as a landlord. They also have a lower buy-in amount, so it's generally cheaper to invest in a REIT than to buy a property.

Investors who invest in REITs are putting up their own cash to invest, like they would invest in a stock or mutual fund. They don't solely own the property, so can't take a mortgage out on it.

The average return on REITs varies depending on the type of REIT you invest in. You're generally investing less money than you would invest when you purchase a property using a down payment and a mortgage, so your returns are generally lower.

Risks for investing in REITS include not having much control over your investment. Unlike when you purchase a house outright, a REIT is controlled by a management team that makes the decisions. Another risk associated with REITs is that there aren't any depreciation write-offs, like there are with investment properties.

It usually takes about one month until you can invest in the REIT, which includes time for due diligence. However, the timeline varies depending on the type of REIT. A private REIT requires investors to keep their investments in the REIT for at least one to two years.

For more information on REITs, read our in-depth guide to investing in REITs.

Tax Lien Investments

Tax liens are a type of real estate investing where investors purchase properties with delinquent tax balances and earn interest and sometimes penalties on the back taxes. They're right for investors who want to earn interest, penalty income and possibly acquire a property for below-market value, the amount of back taxes owed.

Tax lien real estate investing is done with the investor's own resources and is generally paid for with cash. In the event that an investor purchases the tax deed, which means they own the property, they may be able to get financing similar to financing for a property bought at a real estate auction.

The average ROI on tax liens once again varies on the amount of interest and penalties being charged and on the amount of the balance owed. The higher the interest and penalties, generally the higher your ROI will be. Tax lien returns vary widely because in some states, investors "bid down" at auction and their bid determines how much interest they will accept. For example, the interest may start at 16 percent and they may bid down to 4 percent, meaning they will accept 4 percent interest on the tax lien payment.

Some of the risks of investing in tax liens are that the homeowner will repay the debt during the redemption period and reclaim ownership to the house. Another risk is purchasing a property that isn't worth much if you didn't do your due diligence on researching the property. Keep in mind that when a homeowner files bankruptcy, it can halt all collections and affect your penalty income and interest.

The timeline of the tax lien depends on how much time the municipality gives the delinquent homeowner during what is called a redemption period. This is the time that the owner has to pay their tax balance in full plus penalties and/or interest, after the tax lien sale. This varies by municipality and can be a few months or a few years.

For more information on investing in tax liens, check out our in-depth guide to tax lien and tax deed investing.

THE BENEFITS OF INVESTING IN RESIDENTIAL REAL ESTATE

If you're an investor who is worried about getting involved in Real Estate – you're not alone! I can totally understand why some first-time investors get nervous. They've heard ALL the disasters stories that their friends, family, work colleagues and general acquaintances have experienced, and now they're wondering – what if this happens to me too?

There is risk in everything we do, however some risks can be mitigated through the simple process of educating ourselves appropriately.

In the end, it's important to remember that if you do your research, practice due diligence and have the support of key people along the way, your investment is more likely to succeed than not! Well located residential property has an unequalled track record of producing consistent capital growth.

Still not sure if you should invest in Residential Real Estate? Here the top reasons why you should be saying YES!

It's Easy To Learn

Property is relatively easy to learn about. If you find reliable sources, all necessary education is available. Concepts are easy to comprehend and apply to your own situation.

It's Easy To Get Finance

Although sometimes it might not feel like it when it comes to applying for your own mortgage, lenders really do like property! Home loans form a major part of a bank's business model, and statistics show that lenders are more likely to provide finance for residential property than for any other assets – with some offering up to 95% finance, and with lower interest rates than any other type of loans.

It's Flexible

Property is one of the most flexible investments you can make. Regardless of what your financial situation and goals are, there is an investment strategy out there that will suit you.

You Have Control

When it comes to investing in property, you directly own the asset and have complete control over it. This means you can influence both asset worth (by adding value) and cash flow (e.g. by raising the rent) directly. Compared to the share market, where you often need a broker to handle your trades for you, property is a significantly easier asset to manage.

You Can Add Value

There are a number of ways you can increase the value of your property, the most popular of these being renovation. Even small-scale renovations, such as re-painting and landscaping, have the ability to add value to your investment. Larger scale projects, like kitchen remodelling or even removing walls, can add double, if not triple your renovation investment to the value.

There's An Investment For Everyone

Regardless of what your financial situation is or what your budget is, there is a property out there suited to you. There is a common misconception that property is unaffordable for most Australians, however, this is untrue. Sure, not everyone can buy in the prime suburbs of Sydney or Melbourne, but there are many regional towns and cities, cheaper capitals and suburbs away from the city that offer affordable entry points.

You Can Negotiate

When it comes to purchasing most other assets, such as shares, you have no other choice than to buy it for the market price. Property, on the other hand, has more room for negotiation. If you're well versed in the art of negotiation, there's massive potential to get a good deal in price.

Tax Benefits

Come tax time, there are a number of ways property can be advantageous. For example, negative gearing allows you to write off investment expenses against your income. As well as this, you may also benefit from depreciation, which is the decline in value of the property, fixtures and fittings – sometimes this makes the difference between a property being negatively geared and paying for itself.

You Can Invest Using Your Super

Using a Self-Managed Super Fund is one way you might like to invest in property. Capital gains tax on property purchased through a SMSF is 0% if you're over 60.

It's A Tangible Asset

Remember that your property is a physical construct – if anything happens in your life, you can move into the property either long term or short term, and then move out again when things return to normal (of course taking into consideration rental agreements and current tenants).

Others Contribute To Your Investment

Firstly, when financing your investment, you only need to have 5%-20% of the value of the property as a deposit, the rest you can raise from grants or from the bank, depending on your ability to service the loan. Then, when renting out the property to tenants, their rental payments will contribute to or in some cases completely cover the mortgage repayments. Add these factors to the tax benefits you will receive and you're getting 3 separate parties help contribute to your investment!

It's A Long-Term Investment

Depending on the reasons why you have purchased the property, you might like to hang onto it and pass it down to your children. The investment will continue to grow – you don't have to think about it in terms of your lifetime only!

You Can Be As Involved As You Want

If you prefer to sit on the sidelines and let others get their hands dirty instead, good news – nearly everything relating to the property industry is outsourceable! This includes buyer's agents, builders, property managers and more. Hiring professionals is sometimes the best way to ensure you are getting the most out of your investment. On the other hand, if you prefer to do it yourself – whether that be researching properties, being an active landlord or DIY renovations – it's completely possible! When it comes to your investment you are completely in control and can decide how involved or uninvolved you want to be.

7 Major Benefits of Investing in Real Estate

We all, to some extent, recognize the potential financial rewards we could attain from real estate investing. It goes without saying that there are many benefits of investing in real estate that outweigh the costs, and you as a real estate investor could be earning a steady flow of income to secure financial freedom for the long haul.

Whether you want to quit your mundane 9-5 job and become a full time real estate investor and/or save up for your retirement, you are on the right path to fulfill your financial goals sooner than you might think. It takes one rental property to establish your real estate business and get yourself a reliable source of constant rental income.

This year definitely looks promising for investors, and your real estate investments will earn you high returns indeed. The real estate market and the housing conditions are in tip top shape and you can rest assured you will be making money if you invest in the right locations. It is a simple equation: if the economy is growing, the housing market will flourish and there will be an abundance of real estate opportunities to tap into across the country.

Before you set forth with buying your first rental property, make sure you conduct real estate market analysis and consult a real estate professional. If you want to reap financial rewards from investing, you have to make wise and calculated real estate investment decisions in order to grow and diversify your portfolio. Do not depend on luck to win you money in real estate, there is no magic formula, it is all about studying your potential investment before closing any deal. Moreover, if you want to succeed in this industry, you have to know everything about real estate including the benefits you will gain in the short and long term. So let us get started: we will give you 7 major benefits of investing in real estate today.

The Benefits of Real Estate Investing

1. Steady Income

This is a no brainer! The majority of people invest in real estate for the steady flow of cash they earn in the form of rental income. This passive income is a huge incentive to get you started and buy your first rental property. Depending on the location, you could be earning significant income to cover your expenses and make you extra money on the side. Urban cities or towns with colleges and universities tend to reap higher income because the demand is always high in those areas. If chosen wisely, you can secure a steady flow of income for a long time and even save for retirement. And you do not have to stop at investing in one property at a time; you can pick up the pace and invest in multiple rental properties all at once to increase your positive cash flow and diversify your real estate investment portfolio. You can manage by hiring a professional property management professional if the workload becomes too much. One tip to keep in mind: location, location, location is key to smart real estate investing. Don't forget to choose a prime location to reap off the benefits of investing in real estate.

2. Long Term Financial Security

The benefits of investing in real estate provide investors with long term financial security. When you have a steady flow of cash in succession, the rewards of this investment bring on financial rewards for a long time. Owning a rental property can afford investors a sense of security because of the property's appreciation in value over time. This means that your property's value is most likely going to increase because land and buildings are appreciating assets. With that said, however, there is no guarantee the value will increase indefinitely. That is why it is always recommended to thoroughly research the location before closing the deal on the house of choice.

3. Tax Benefits

One of the benefits of investing in real estate is the tax exemptions investors get from owning a rental property. This is a major reason why many choose to invest in real estate. For example, rental income is not subject to self-employment tax. In addition, the government offers tax breaks for property depreciation, insurance, maintenance repairs, travel expenses, legal fees, and property taxes. Real estate investors are also entitled to lower tax rates for their long term investments. Icing on the cake!

4. Mortgage Payments Are Covered

The benefits of investing in real estate include your tenants as well. Simply put, the rental income you receive each month is more than enough to cover your expenses, including your mortgage payments. Essentially, your tenant is actually the one paying your mortgage. That is why it is important to keep your tenants happy and avoid or mitigate the negative repercussions of vacancy at all cost.

5. Real Estate Appreciation

If you already are in real estate investment or are just starting out, you do understand that real estate is not a short term investment plan. On the contrary, the benefits of investing in real estate include the appreciation of capital assets (aka land) over time. In other words, your property's value will be worth way more 30 years from now, hence why investors are in it for the long run.

6. Inflation

One of the benefits of investing in real estate is a hedge against inflation. With high inflation, your rental income and property value increase significantly. Real estate investors welcome inflation with open arms because as the cost of living goes up, so does their cash flow.

7. You Are Your Own Decision Maker

Forget about your 9-5 boring job, the best part about real estate is becoming your own boss. Just like any other business, you have the complete autonomy and control over your real estate investment strategies as well as your failures and successes. You call the shots on which property to invest in, the tenants who will live under your roof, how much rental income to charge per month, and who will manage and maintain the property as a whole. The benefits of investing in real estate make you your own decision maker.

THE BENEFITS OF INVESTING IN REAL ESTATE VS. OTHER INVESTMENT OPPORTUNITIES

Do you know the benefits of investing in real estate? Have you ever thought about how the rich seem to make growing their wealth look easy? Do you think you will be able to retire comfortably when the time comes? Perhaps even more importantly; are you aware that you should invest, but just don't know where to begin?

If you answered "yes" to any of the previous questions, there is a good chance that you have a lot more questions of your own. Today's financial world is as equally intimidating as it is intriguing. However, with the right insight, investing can be one of the most lucrative endeavors you partake in. Real estate investing, in particular, has proven – time and time again – that it can serve as a wealth-building vehicle for savvy investors. Our partners at CT Homes have flipped hundreds of properties in every market condition, proving definitively that real estate is a viable investment strategy.

The following was created to help you understand some of the investment opportunities made available to you, and why we think investing in real estate is the superior option:

5 Undeniable Real Estate Benefits

Tax Advantages: Taxes are one of the biggest expenses for anyone – let alone a real estate investment company. However, there are ways to combat the loss of money in taxes with real estate. Rental houses, apartments, vacant land, commercial buildings, industrial, shopping centers and warehouses all offer their own variation of tax incentives.

Cash Flow: Perhaps everyone's favorite benefit, cash flow is essentially profit. Cash flow is what is left over after you collect the rent and pay your mortgage, taxes, insurance and any repairs.

Hedge Against Inflation: Inflation is defined as a sustained increase in the general level of prices for goods and services. In other words, it causes every dollar you own to buy a smaller percentage of a good or service over time. Stocks, for instance, require more money to purchase with the increase of inflation. Essentially, inflation prevents your money from going as far as it would have. Real estate, on the other hand, serves as a hedge against inflation. Unlike almost every other form of investment, real estate reacts proportionately to inflation. As inflation increases, so too do rents and home values.

Leverage Funds: When purchasing a property, you have the ability to do so with leverage. It is entirely possible to purchase a $500,000 property with $100,000. You don't even have to use your own money. Stocks, on the other hand, require 100 percent of the investment up front. Leveraging money also allows you to initiate more than one real estate deal at a time because all of your funds aren't tied up in one project.

Equity: In the event you borrow money to complete a real estate deal, you will be required to pay it back with interest. However, each payment also gets you one step closer to paying down your principal payments. You are simultaneously building equity and wealth in the same property.

Invest In Real Estate Vs. Stock Market

The minute you decide to take the plunge and buy stocks, you will find yourself as the partial owner of a respective company – regardless of how small your share may be. As the company's earnings improve, so will your stock. Savvy investors may be rewarded in the form of appreciation and dividends. In fact, since 1945, the average large stock has returned close to 10 percent a year. Stocks really can serve as a long-term savings vehicle. That said, stocks could just as easily depreciate. They are by no means a sure thing.

Not unlike real estate, playing the stock market has become synonymous with high returns for those that know what they are doing. However, it is just that: playing a game. The stock market is as much out of your control as anything can be. If you invest in stocks, you will be at the mercy of a relatively volatile market. That said, real estate is the polar opposite in regards to certain aspects. Net earnings in real estate are reflective of your own actions. You are really in control of your own money. Any money gained or lost is a direct result of what you do.

Bonds Vs. Real Estate

Stocks and bonds, while often lumped together, are fundamentally different from one another. Unlike stocks, bonds are not representative of a stake in a company. As a result, the return on a bond is fixed and does not have the opportunity to appreciate. Bonds function as a loan that is paid back by a company over time with interest. This, of course, makes bonds less volatile than stocks. However, bonds are not liquid and do not offer the same returns as most other investments. While bonds are relatively safe, they do not offer impressive returns like other investment strategies.

Typically, the safer the bond, the lower the interest rate of return. However, invested in carefully, real estate can rival the safety of bonds with a much higher return. The real advantage real estate holds over bonds is the time frame for holding the investments and the rate of return during that time. Bonds pay a fixed rate of interest over the life of the investment, thus purchasing power with that interest drops with inflation over time. Rental property, on the other hand, can generate higher rents in periods of higher inflation.

Real Estate Vs. Gold

Most people invest in gold for its popularity. It is as simple as that. There will always be a demand for the precious metal, as "Fifty percent of the world's population believes in gold."

However, demand pressure is expected to increase in the latter parts of 2015. As a result, gold prices should come back down to earth. This should attract inventors looking to capitalize on the ground level.

Recognized as a relatively safe commodity, gold has established itself as a vehicle to increase investment returns. However, there are those that don't even consider gold to be an investment at all, rather a hedge against inflation. The precious metal acts as a way to protect wealth against the risk of loss in select asset classes.

Of course, as safe as gold may be considered, it still fails to remain as attractive as real estate. Here are a few reasons investors prefer real estate over gold:

Unlike real estate, there is no financing and, therefore, no room to leverage for growth.

Unlike real estate, gold proposes no tax advantages.

In contrast to real estate rental, there is no income potential.

If gold does go up in value, the gain is nominal rather than an actual increase in buying power.

Real Estate Vs. Certificates of Deposit (CDs)

Certificates of deposit, or CDs if you will, operate a lot like savings accounts. Seeing as how they are backed, they are virtually risk-free. Of course, unlike savings accounts, CDs offer a specific, fixed-term and interest rate. This form of investment is intended to be held till it matures, which can be anywhere from three months to five years, typically. When the CD matures, you can collect the original investment, along with some interest. Certificates of deposit do not appreciate in value, and they've had a historical average return of 2.84 percent in the last eleven years. Real estate, on the other hand, can appreciate in value.

Real Estate Vs. Mutual Funds

As their names suggest, mutual funds consist of finances that have been pooled together. The money is then invested into a variety of asset types: stocks, bonds, similar mutual funds, and commodities like gold or fine art. It is one of the easiest ways to diversify any portfolio.

The performance of a mutual fund is always measured in terms of total return, or the sum of the change in a fund's net asset value (NAV), its dividends and its capital gains distributions over a given period of time.

However, much like stocks, you have little control over the performance of your assets. Future investment performance is subject to many variables. In fact, placing money into a mutual fund is essentially handing one's investment decisions over to a professional money manager. While you can pick and choose your investments, you have little say over how they perform.

THE INCREDIBLE TAX BENEFITS OF REAL ESTATE INVESTING

Real Estate Business vs Investment

As fledgling real estate investors, we had two challenges. First, we had to use real estate to make a living. Second, we had to use real estate to build wealth so that we could achieve financial independence.

To make a living we got into the real estate business. We learned how to find and quickly resell deals for a profit. Sometimes we sold these in as-is condition to other investors (aka wholesaling). Other times we fixed them up and sold them to end-users (aka retailing).

To build wealth and retire early, we also began buying real estate investments. We wanted our investments to grow and fund our early retirement with regular, steady income. Luckily, real estate has many different strategies to do both of those very well.

How to Make Money in Real Estate.

Without profits, tax benefits are not relevant. So, let's first look at how you make money in real estate investing.

Just remember that real estate is an I.D.E.A.L. investment:

Income: Regular cash flow from rents or interest payments. I consistently see unleveraged returns of 5-10% from this one method of making money. With reasonable leverage, it's possible to see these returns jump to the 10-15% range or better.

Depreciation: A required accounting method that spreads the cost of an asset over multiple years (27.5 years for residential real estate). This paper expense can "shelter" or protect other income from taxes and reduce your tax bill. I'll explain depreciation in more detail later.

Equity: If you borrow money to buy a rental property, your tenant essentially pays off the property for you. You use the rent to pay the mortgage, and each month the principal paydown (aka equity) gets bigger and bigger like a forced savings account.

Appreciation: Over the long-run real estate has gone up in value about the same rate as inflation (3-4%). This passive style of inflation helps, but active appreciation is even more profitable. Active appreciation happens when you force the value higher over a shorter period of time, like with a house remodel.

Leverage: Many investors use debt leverage to buy real estate. This means, for example, $100,000 can buy four properties at $25,000 down instead of just one property for $100,000. Leverage magnifies the profits mentioned above (and potentially the losses). Plus, interest on debt is deductible as a business expense.

Not every real estate deal has every one of these profit centers. And sometimes you have to give up one in order to get another.

For example, one time I purchased a mobile home on land. I paid cash (so no leverage and no equity growth). The mobile home itself went down in value like a car (negative appreciation). But the income was excellent. And the depreciation sheltered some of the income from taxes.

Another investment was a more expensive single family house in a great neighborhood. Initially, the net rent after expenses barely paid the mortgage (no income). But my equity built up quickly because the loan amortized quickly. And the property was in a great location likely to appreciate at or above the overall inflation rate.

Now you know the basic ways to make money. Let's move on to 10 different tax benefits of investing in real estate.

1. Depreciation Shelters Income From Tax

The IRS uses depreciation to acknowledge that an asset wears down over time. Somehow they discovered that residential real estate wears down in exactly 27.5 years (sarcasm intended). Other assets have different timelines.

Unlike other business expenses, depreciation is a paper loss. This means you don't spend any money, yet you still get the expense. This expense can offset taxable income and save money on your tax bill.

Here is a basic example:

Scenario 1 (without depreciation expense):

$5,000 taxable rental income x 25% federal income tax rate = $1,250 taxes owed

Scenario 2 (with depreciation expense):

$5,000 rental income – $3,000 depreciation expense = $2,000 taxable rental income

$2,000 x 25% federal income tax rate = $500 taxes owed

Tax Savings = $1,250 – $500 = $750

The higher your tax rate, the more taxes you would save in this example.

Depreciation is not unique to real estate, but real estate investing uniquely benefits from depreciation. Why?

Because the cost of real estate is so large and often purchased with debt.

A $200,000 building depreciated over 27.5 years provides tax shelter of $7,272 per year. If you had 3 rental properties, you'd shelter $21,816 of income from taxes and possibly* save $5,454 on your tax bill (at a 25% rate)!

2. Avoid FICA (Payroll) Tax on Rental Income

Just like dividends and interest income, rental income is not subject to social security and medicare taxes (aka FICA). While this is not an enormous benefit when compared to other investments, it is significant when compared to normal earned income.

If you earn money at a normal salaried job, you pay 7.65% (as of 2016) of your salary in FICA taxes. If you're self-employed, you pay 15.3% towards FICA tax.

With a $100,000 salary, that's $7,650 or $15,300 out of pocket from your salary. But if you earn $100,000 in rental income, you avoid the tax completely. This is a big incentive to start earning your money from rental income.

3. No Tax On Appreciation (aka Buy & Hold Like Buffett)

One of the most tax-efficient methods to build wealth is simply not selling. "My favorite holding period is forever."

When you sell, you pay transaction fees, commissions, and taxes. All of these costs drag down your long-term performance because you forever lose the ability for those dollars to compound and grow.

And real estate appreciation doesn't get taxed by the IRS. So, if you buy and hold for many years it's possible to let your net worth grow with minimal tax exposure.

And when you do choose to sell, real estate has other benefits.

4. Capital Gains Tax at Lower Rates

As of 2016, long-term capital gains tax rates are between 0% to 25%, depending upon your tax bracket. Of course, the shifting political climate can always change these rates. But in general capital gains tax rates are lower than ordinary income tax rates.

Low capital gains rates are an advantage if you build your long-term investment strategy around strategically selling real estate for growth or living expenses.

For example, one year my deductions and rental depreciation placed me into the second lowest tax bracket. I sell several properties that year, so my long-term capital gain tax rate was 0%!

But even in the higher brackets of 15% or 20%, capital gains tax would have been better than the equivalent income tax on ordinary income.

5. Live In Your Flip = No Taxes

What if you want to avoid capital gains tax altogether? Then just buy and immediately move into the house as your principle residence. As long as you live in the home 2 out of the next 5 years, in the U.S. you can make a tax-free profit of up to $250,000 as an individual or $500,000 as a couple. Canada and the U.K. have slightly different rules, but the principle is the same.

A real estate strategy called the Live-In Flip takes advantage of this generous tax exemption. Carl from 1500days.com wrote an awesome guest post for me explaining how several live-in flips built enormous wealth and accelerated his path to early retirement.

Keep in mind that this doesn't have to be a permanent strategy. You could do 2 or 3 flips, reinvest the earnings, and move on to other investment strategies.

6. Exchange Properties For Tax-Free Growth

Another way to avoid capital gains tax (and also depreciation recapture tax) is a section 1031 tax-free exchange. This technique is named after section 1031 of the U.S. tax code.

A 1031 exchange allows you to trade one property for another without paying taxes. You must follow specific rules, and you must be classified as an investor (i.e. not a dealer who flips houses).

Why is this helpful? Because you get to use 100% of the profits from the sale to reinvest in the next property. This maximizes the growth and compounding of your investments.

For example, let's say you sell a property for $300,000 without a 1031 exchange and pay $35,000 in capital gain and depreciation recapture taxes. By avoiding these taxes using a 1031 exchange, you would keep that $35,000 invested. At 10% for the next 20 years, that $35,000 would grow to over $235,000!

I must admit that I've not yet had the need to do 1031 exchange in my own real estate investing. The fees and rigid process make it difficult (and expensive) to execute, and I've been able to take advantage of the other tax savings I've mentioned in this book. But 1031 exchanges can still make a lot of sense for many investors.

7. Installment Sales For Income & Deferred Taxes

The IRS gives property investors another tool to reduce taxes on the sale of real estate. This tool is called an installment sale (aka seller financing or seller carry-back mortgage).

Like 1031 exchanges, installment sales are only available to property investors and not to dealers (house flippers). Also like 1031 exchanges, installment sales allow an investor to defer capital gains tax, but unfortunately the entire amount of accumulated depreciation must be recaptured at the initial time of sale.

From a practical standpoint, an installment sale just means the seller of an investment property receives the sales price over time. The seller is essentially extending credit to the buyer instead of the buyer getting a bank loan (here is my visual explanation on YouTube).

For example, a duplex owner could sell me her property for $300,000. $30,000 could be a down payment, and I would still owe $270,000 in the form of a seller financing mortgage. The terms of the financing might be $1,934 per month at 6% for 20 years.

This arrangement would be most beneficial if the duplex owner owned the property for a long time and experienced a huge run-up in prices. For example, my duplex owner might have bought the property for $50,000 over 30 years ago.

An installment sale would allow this owner to only pay taxes on the profits received each year. A $250,000 gain at one time would have pushed the seller into higher tax brackets. But the installment sale allows the seller to slowly receive the gains and possibly stay in lower, more favorable tax brackets.

It's also worth mentioning that installment sales can be a great way to transition out of active property management and into a period of more passive income.

8. Borrow Tax-Free Instead of Sell

To raise cash most investors consider selling investments. As I've shown above, this exposes you to taxes or complicated procedures to avoid tax. But with real estate you have another choice. You can simply pull capital out of an investment tax-free by refinancing.

9. Self-Directed IRA Real Estate Investing

IRAs and 401k style retirement plans are incredible tools to build wealth while minimizing taxes. But most people think of them only as tools to invest in traditional investments like stocks, bonds, mutual funds, and REITs. While this is the norm, it's not the rule.

The IRS does not describe what your IRA account can invest in. It only describes what you can NOT invest in. The "do not invest list" includes life insurance and collectibles like artwork, rugs, and antiques. Non-traditional investments like real estate, private mortgages, limited partnerships, and tax liens are therefore allowed. But most larger retirement account custodians (i.e. Vanguard, Schwab, etc) do not choose to offer them as a possibility.

So, there is an entire industry of specialized custodians who do allow investments in these non-traditional assets. A google search will give you dozens of possibilities.

While self-directed IRAs are a wonderful tool, there are many pitfalls and strict rules to be careful of. For example, you can't self-deal by loaning money to yourself or to another disqualified person, like a close family member. If you break one of the rules, you could face large penalties and disqualification of your account from tax-free status.

My favorite way to invest with my IRA is a loan against real estate. It's lower risk and has fewer moving parts than actually owning the real estate itself.

10. Die With Real Estate (Seriously)

This may sound like a joke, but one of the best plans (at least as a tax strategy!) is to die with your real estate. Instead of facing the tax issues of recaptured depreciation or capital gains tax, your heirs instead get a stepped-up basis.

For example, let's say you bought a rental house for $100,000. Forty years later you die and the house is worth $500,000. When your heirs sell the house, they would not pay capital gains tax on the $400,000 gain. Instead, their basis would be $500,000, which means they could sell it for $500,000 and have no capital gains tax to pay.

Keep in mind that inherited assets are still subject to estate taxes. But as of this writing (2016) $5.45 million of assets are exempt from any estate taxes. So, your heirs would inherit a lot of property before paying any taxes.

Of course, you don't have to let the tail wag the dog. Tax benefits are only part of the overall equation of finances in your life. You may have plenty of legitimate reasons (like enjoyment of life!) to pay taxes and spend the money before you die. You could also contribute a portion of your assets to charity, still pay no taxes, and help decide how worthwhile causes will benefit from your wealth while you're alive.

As you have seen, tax benefits are a compelling reason to get involved in real estate. But tax benefits are never the sole reason to invest in real estate or anything else. Basic economics and quality of your investments are primary factors to consider when choosing your strategy.

And you also need to make sure real estate fits your lifestyle. I think real estate is often overlooked as a viable retirement strategy, especially by early retirees. But it's clearly not for everyone. Do your homework and figure out what's best for you. And if you choose to invest in real estate, be sure to build a team of professionals to support you. One of the most important team members will be a tax professional like a CPA or qualified tax attorney. All of the strategies I've mentioned here are a start, but a professional can help you apply the details to your situation.

CHAPTER THREE

10 HABITS OF SUCCESSFUL REAL ESTATE INVESTORS

Joint ventures, wholesaling and property management are just a few of the ways investors can profit from real estate, but it takes a little savvy to become successful in this competitive arena. While certain universities offer coursework and programs that specifically benefit real estate investors, a degree is not necessarily a prerequisite to profitable real estate investing. Whether an investor has a degree or not, there are certain characteristics that top real estate investors commonly possess. Here are the 10 habits that highly effective real estate investors share.

1. Make a Plan

Real estate investors must approach their real estate activities as a business in order to establish and achieve short- and long-term goals. A business plan also allows investors to visualize the big picture, which helps maintain focus on the goals rather than on any minor setbacks. Real estate investing can be complicated and demanding, and a solid plan can keep investors organized and on task.

2. Know the Market

Effective real estate investors acquire an in-depth knowledge of their selected market(s). Keeping abreast of current trends — including any changes in consumer spending habits, mortgage rates and the unemployment rate, to name a few — lets real estate investors acknowledge current conditions and plan for the future. This enables them to predict when trends may change, creating potential opportunities for the prepared investor.

3. Be Honest

Real estate investors are usually not obligated to uphold a particular degree of ethics. Although it would be easy to take advantage of this situation, most successful real estate investors maintain high ethical standards. Since real estate investing involves people, an investor's reputation is likely to be far reaching. Effective real estate investors know it is better to be fair, rather than to see what they can get away with.

4. Develop a Niche

It is important for investors to develop a focus in order to gain the depth of knowledge essential to becoming successful. Taking the time to build this level of understanding of a specific area is integral to long-term success. Once a particular market is mastered, the investor can move on to additional areas using the same in-depth approach.

5. Encourage Referrals

Referrals generate a sizable portion of a real estate investor's business, so it is critical that investors treat others with respect. This includes business partners, associates, clients, renters and anyone with whom the investor has a business relationship. Effective real estate investors pay attention to detail, listen and respond to complaints and concerns, and represent their business in a positive and professional manner. This builds the kind of reputation that makes others interested in working with those investors.

6. Stay Educated

As with any business, it is imperative to stay up to date with the laws, regulations, terminology and trends that form the basis of the real estate investor's business. Investors who fall behind risk not only losing momentum in their businesses, but also legal ramifications if laws are ignored or broken. Successful real estate investors stay educated and adapt to any regulatory changes or economic trends.

7. Understand the Risks

Stock or futures market investors are inundated with warnings regarding the inherent risks involved in investing. Real estate investors, however, are more likely to see advertisements claiming just the opposite: that it is easy to make money in real estate. Prudent real estate investors understand the risks – not only in terms of real estate deals, but also the legal implications involved – and adjust their businesses to reduce those risks.

8. Invest in an Accountant

Taxes comprise a significant portion of a real estate investor's yearly expenses. Understanding current tax laws can be complicated and take time away from the business at hand. Sharp real estate investors retain the services of a qualified, reputable accountant to handle the business's books. The costs associated with the accountant can be negligible when compared to the savings a professional can bring to the business.

9. Find Help

Learning the real estate investing business is challenging to someone attempting to do things on their own. Effective real estate investors often attribute part of their success to others – whether a mentor, lawyer or supportive friend. Rather than risk time and money tackling a difficult problem alone, successful real estate investors know it is worth the additional costs (in terms of money and ego) to embrace other people's expertise.

10. Build a Network

A network can provide important support and create opportunities for both new and experienced real estate investors. This type of group – comprised of a well-chosen mentor, business partners, clients or members of a non-profit organization – allows investors to challenge and support one another. Because much of real estate investing relies on experiential learning, savvy real estate investors understand the importance of building a network.

Despite abundant advertisements claiming that real estate investing is an easy way to wealth, it is in fact a challenging business requiring expertise, planning and focus. In addition, because the business revolves around people, investors benefit in the long run by operating with integrity and by showing respect to associates and clients. Though it may be relatively simple to earn short-lived profits, developing a long-term real estate investing business requires skill, effort and these 10 important habits.

8 PITFALLS TO AVOID WHEN INVESTING IN RESIDENTIAL REAL ESTATE

One of the richest people of all time, Andrew Carnegie, once said "90% of all millionaires become so through real estate investing." Real estate has proven to be a successful method of building wealth for centuries, but that doesn't mean you can just buy a property and expect to be a millionaire the next day. There is a right way and a wrong way to purchase real estate, and if you're not careful, you could find yourself falling into a very large pit.

Here are eight popular pitfalls that investors often face when investing in real estate:

Pitfall 1: Chasing the Highest Yield

Some investors focus too heavily on one number – yield and the highest they can get. There is nothing wrong with investing in high-yield properties, but focusing solely on the yields can cause you to overlook important factors that affect profit.

As with investing in any asset class, there is always a balance between risk-and-reward. And those properties with the highest yields often come with the highest risks. This typically comes from higher tenant turnover, vacancies, and costly renovations. "Investors need to realize that higher-yielding properties are great for real estate experts that have the time to manage their own assets and understand local laws,""The goal for our investors is to help them make successful choices when it comes to their real estate investing, so they can achieve positive results, not just high yields."

How to Avoid: If you are going to chase the highest-yielding properties then you need to be prepared. This means allocating large chunks of your budget to renovations and preparing ahead for months of no cash flow due to unpredicted vacancies. An alternate solution would be to invest in properties in good neighborhoods that have stable returns, albeit with a slightly lower yield.

Pitfall 2: Waiting for an Unrealistic Opportunity

Real estate investors have been capitalizing on strong markets around the country, many of which are seeing new highs. On the other side of the equation are investors who are standing by, waiting for the perfect investment property to appear.

This "perfect opportunity" stems from a very specific picture of how an income property will look and feel, and even where it will be located. Investors often picture a turnkey property with very high yields, a great school district, and stable tenants. This perfect investment property is extremely rare in this tight housing market, and if you wait, all you will be doing is letting your money sit idly, while others prosper in real estate investing.

How to Avoid: Instead of waiting for the perfect investment property to fall into your lap, focus on finding the right investment property for you. Finding the right property means looking at a neighborhood that presents the right risk-versus-reward for your goals. This means coming in with realistic expectations for yields based on what you are trying to achieve; for instance, someone closer to retirement, should be looking to maximize their income today in a low-risk neighborhood. In comparison, someone with a 20+ year retirement horizon can look for properties with more of a balance of risk-and-reward.

Pitfall 3: Thinking You'll get Rich Quick

Another popular pitfall that many new investors find themselves falling into is looking at real estate investing as a way to get rich quick. While you can certainly successfully invest in income properties with a solid ROI, expecting real estate to lead to riches overnight will leave you thoroughly disappointed.

An exception to this pitfall is fix and flip, since it has a much quicker timeline to generate income, if performed successfully. That being said, a majority of fix and flips are fix and fails that require a ton of work from the investor. This work includes hiring contractors, managing the rehab, designing the renovations, and more. In this current market of low homeownership rates and increasing rents, buy-and-hold strategy is definitely the better way to go.

How to Avoid: In order to maximize your gains from real estate, it should be viewed as a long-term investment, or buy-and-hold strategy. Monthly cash flow can be generated through rents, but profits can also be found on the property through appreciation.

Pitfall 4: Not Accounting for Enough of the Costs

Part of the research that comes with finding and purchasing a quality investment property is evaluating all the costs. While it is easiest to only look at the large yield percentage and not factor a realistic scenario of the overall investment, your ROI is very important.

How to Avoid: While each property is unique, you have to account for many of the costs that all rental properties will face. This includes costs like vacancies between tenants, maintenance, and repairs. Additionally, there are other fees such as HOA, taxes, leasing fees, property management, and insurance, which can all affect your bottom-line. Calculating these costs in advance can help you plan accordingly and know what kind of realistic profits to expect.

Pitfall 5: Focusing too Heavily on the Appearance of the Investment Property

The old saying goes that we can't "judge a book by its cover" and that is a pitfall that many investors find themselves being stuck in when it comes to residential real estate. Just because a property might have been the victim of bad lighting or pictures taken from an amateur, it shouldn't be the overall deciding factor, if it is a good investment or not.

See the example above that shows how photos can sometimes be deceiving when it comes to real estate. Based off the before photos, an investor may have overlooked this investment property, which would have been a big mistake. After the renovation, as you can see in the After photos, this property tenanted quickly and received the full monthly rent projection of $980.

How to Avoid: Look past the outside appearance of a property, as this can help you see a property's true potential. A little rehab can go a long way and help you maximize your profits by attracting the right tenants. Often times, a simple rehab of minor changes to flooring, paint, or even small repairs can lead to a significant difference in rent potential. Also, remember you are not living in the home; it's purely an investment opportunity. With the right attitude, you can combat this pitfall.

Pitfall 6: Buying Just Because a Tenant is in Place

Investing in a property with a tenant already in place can be a serious motivator for investors. Although this means that cash flow is likely coming-in on day one, managing these types of properties might not always be as clear cut as it looks. Often times these properties come with tenants that are more than you bargained for, such as delinquent on the rent, not making enough income to pay, or they come with a poor rent payment history that could led to possible eviction later on. And the worst part? The seller probably failed to mention any of these issues with the tenant.

How to Avoid: As an investment firm that helps investors find, acquire, and manage residential real estate, we've had a very personal experience with Pitfall #6. In clear transparency, when we first started providing properties with tenants in place for our investors, we noticed a serious problem. 23% of these tenanted properties came with 60 to 90-days delinquent tenants. The previous third-party owner did not mention this upfront. This led us to create and implement a thorough screening process for tenants already living in the home before we made any recommendations to our investors. Make sure you do your homework on the tenant before purchasing rental properties with a tenant already in place, or buy an untenanted property and put in a reliable tenant from the get-go by using our proven screening methods.

Pitfall 7: Limiting Yourself to Your Own Backyard

When looking for locations to invest in residential real estate, many investors simply look to their own backyard. While there might be some good investments nearby, you could be missing out on better investment opportunities across the country, especially if home prices in your neighborhood are high.

How to Avoid: Remote investing allows you to purchase residential real estate in markets throughout the U.S., therefore making it easier to find properties that fit your investment goals, initial investment amount, and more. By working with a partner who will help you find these markets as well as manage the properties, you'll reap the benefits. This means investing in markets that are poised for growth, have higher cap rates, and/or have a solid cash-on-cash return.

Pitfall 8: Doing it by Yourself

Some investors choose to take on the entire investment process on their own, but this is a huge hazard. While it is certainly possible to find, acquire, and manage your rental properties by yourself, there are benefits to working with real estate investing experts. Additionally, there are many roles that play a part in the investment process including real estate agents, lenders, contractors, property managers, and other highly specialized roles.

How to Avoid: Just like you would research different properties, the same principle applies to the groups you work with. Working with the right parties can help you achieve your investing goals, and provide expertise on the real estate investing process.

Also, working with the right management company can make sure that you don't have to oversee all the daily details with your tenants. A good property management company will help you find tenants, collect rents, and take care of any repairs.

The Best Way to Avoid Pitfalls, and Leap to Success

Carnegie and many others have used real estate to help them grow their capital, and you can too. Although many investors fall into the pitfalls above, you won't, since you've learned what you need to avoid, and how working with an expert partner can help ensure your success.

6 ADVANTAGES OF REAL ESTATE INVESTING FOR SAVVY ENTREPRENEURS

I've had numerous conversations with entrepreneurs lately who have come to the conclusion that they need to start diversifying their business profits into more than just a savings account. If this is you - pay close attention.

Being a real estate investor isn't always glamorous but it is one of the best ways to build wealth over the long-haul, especially for the entrepreneurial-minded. Here are six reasons why you should consider investing in rental properties.

1. Cash flow.

Many people invest in rental properties simply because of the cash flow - the extra money that is left after all the bills have been paid. The cash flow can provide ongoing, monthly income that is mostly passive, allowing you to spend your time building a business, traveling or reinvesting in more real estate.

Cash flow from real estate is stable and far more predictable than most other businesses. That's great for entrepreneurs enduring the ups and downs of start-up life. The cash flow can help float you though the bad times and live well during the good times.

2. Tax benefits.

Let me ask you a quick question: if you earn $100,000 at your own business and I earn $100,000 through rental properties, who get's to keep more?

That's right: I do. Because the government rewards rental property owners.

Not only is the cash flow received from your rentals not subject to self-employment tax, the government offers tax benefits including depreciation and significantly lower tax-rates for long-term profits.

3. The loan pay down.

When you buy a rental property using a mortgage, your tenant is actually the one paying the mortgage payment, thus increasing your net worth each month. Because of the loan pay down a rental property is essentially a savings account that grows automatically, without you depositing money each month.

Today you might owe $200,000 on a rental property, but next year you might only owe $195,000 because the tenant is making the payment for you, making you $5,000 richer. Thirty years down the road, or whatever the term of your loan, it's paid down to $0. You own a significant asset that you can sell or continue renting, all thanks to your tenant paying the mortgage.

4. Appreciation.

While the loan is being paid down the value of real estate, generally, goes up. Yes, I know, recessions do happen. Values do go up and down. People buy at the wrong time of the market.

5. A hedge against inflation.

Can you imagine paying ten dollars for a gallon of milk? Or five dollars for a candy bar? While those prices seem exorbitant to you, this is the future because of inflation.

Inflation is the process by which prices increase due to the value of money decreasing.

While most people fear inflation, as a rental property owner, I look forward to it!

When the price of a gallon of milk hits ten bucks a gallon, guess what else is going to shoot through the roof? Everything, including rents and property values! The one thing that won't increase, however, is my fixed-rate mortgage payment. As inflation pushes the cost of living higher and higher, my cash flow will only increase. This is why real estate is often called "a hedge against inflation." When inflation hits - I'm ready!

6. Control.

If values drop, I can choose to wait it out or improve the property to drive the value back up.

In other words, I get to control the situation, and my financial future, with my own two hands. And that suits me just fine.

Don't think that just by owning some rentals you are instantly going to begin building wealth. Real estate is powerful - but only if you work it right.

THE ADVANTAGES OF INVESTING IN COMMERCIAL REAL ESTATE TODAY

Real estate has been a popular source of investment for investors of a backgrounds and financial standings. It's safe, secure, and offers the potential for great returns. Given the volatility of other markets in the current economy, the property arena is perhaps an even more attractive than ever. While all opportunities in this field are good, there's no doubt that commercial real estate is the best.

Commercial investments hold many advantages over residential real estate. This is in addition to non-property related opportunities. Here are the most attractive elements that should pull you towards this marketplace.

Profit Potential

Revenue should be at the heart of all investment ventures, which is why commercial real estate is one of the greatest options on the market. The growing demand for commercial spaces throughout Louisville is key. It allows property investors and developers to see their capital grow at a far better rate than other opportunities. As a long-term investment, commercial properties offer the potential for huge progress.

Commercial property value reflects the rental costs too. So if the asset's rental value increases 50%, it's worth will follow suit. This means that the inflation will often outweigh that of other properties. Better still, the return on investment becomes evident as soon as you find tenants for those units. Whether monthly, quarterly or annually, this regular stream of income aids ongoing cash flow.

All investors are primarily concerned with the potential yields. For this reason alone, commercial properties should be on the shortlist for all potential investors. Check out what commercial properties are available today.

Easier Management

Residential properties do offer plenty of benefits. However, the life of a landlord isn't always easy. Not only is there a threat of bad tenants to consider, but there's also a need to provide the right facilities for each tenant. With commercial properties, though, the management aspects are far less stressful. This enables you to play a more passive role in the investment.

When you own several units in the same location, an onsite manager can take care of virtually all operational issues. Meanwhile, any maintenance contractors will often offer discounts due to working on a large number of properties at once. Essentially, this means that the operational costs per property are lower than the alternatives. More importantly, the investment will consume only a small percentage of your time.

This subsequently opens greater versatility in terms of the portfolio. A diverse group of offices, stores, hotels, etc. can only boost the hopes of securing a high ROI too.

Flexibility Of Funding

Commercial property also offers a chance to procure a portfolio of assets far greater than the initial outlay. This is due largely to the flexibility of funding, which is gained from the fact you needn't buy properties with cash. In most situations, the down payment can be as little as 20%.

This means that you can potentially gain assets of up to 5x your current wealth. In turn, this offers a fantastic opportunity for leverage and continued growth. When coupled with the inflation gained from the fact that properties reflect rental value, the appeal isn't hard to see.

Commercial real estate needn't always be a solo investment either. There are many opportunities to use co-ownership and joint ventures. This reduces the initial outlay and pressure while ensuring you have two brains working on the same venture.

Tax Benefits For Maximum Returns

Investments can be a complex environment. Sadly, it's not as black and white as simply generating profits. Commercial efforts may also be influenced by taxes and other external factors. When dealing with properties, those elements can actually be used to your gain.

The asset may grow in terms of its market value and financial worth to you, the investor. However, the building itself is sure to encounter depreciation over the years. Straight line depreciation shows that a property's physical worth will depreciate over 27.5 years. Meanwhile, other aspects may drop in under a decade. This loss can be offset against the market value profits, resulting in a better outcome in reality.

Those elements will require a professional accountant. Still, those opportunities aren't available in most markets. This is yet another reason to choose commercial real estate over other solutions.

Optimum Control

Ultimately, those investment ventures are designed to enhance your life. Therefore, you don't simply need the flexibility over the acquisition of assets. You also need to think about potential exit strategies. Again, the demand for commercial real estate, not least in Louisville, makes it a great avenue.

Most commercial real estate investors will manage multiple properties, even in those early days. When circumstances dictate that money is required, moving some units on is not an issue. This can free up money, and usually in a far quicker time than residential properties, without quitting the arena altogether.

This sense of control can be very comforting, even when you aren't in a position where it's needed. As an investor, taking those indirect factors into account is key.

Reduced Risks

The very nature of investment opportunities means that there will always be a degree of risk involved. As a responsible investor, minimizing those possible dangers is essential. As all of the above points above highlight, commercial real estate offers one of the most secure solutions on the market.

Unlike investing in company shares, property ownership ensures that you have tangible assets. History shows that even global giants are capable of suffering major blows or failing altogether. Having hard assets prevents that from happening. In the immediate future, it's unlikely that commercial properties in Louisville will be on the market without interest for long.

On a similar note, owning several units means that the reliance on each one is reduced. If one is unused, its impact on revenue is minimal. Compare this to the impact that an uninhabited house can cause for a landlord, and it's not hard to see why commercial beats residential.

The Final Word

There are no 100% guarantees in this world. Still, as far as modern investments in the Louisville area are concerned, commercial real estate is as close as you'll get. With the right advice and support, success is virtually assured.

CHAPTER FOUR

HOW REAL ESTATE INVESTMENTS RETURN PROFITS

When you purchase a company's stock certificates, you're looking for appreciation in the stock value, and perhaps dividend income, if the company pays it. With bonds, you're looking for income yield on the interest rate paid by the bonds. With a real estate investments, there are even more ways in which to realize a superior return on investment. Learn the ways in which your real estate investment can increase in value, as well as provide good cash flow.

Cash Flow From Rental Income

As is the case with a stock that pays dividends, a properly selected and managed rental property can provide a steady income stream in the form of rental payments. Rental property returns typically exceed dividend yields.

Real estate investors also have more control over risks to their cash flow. Though there are slumps in real estate prices and slow markets, people who own residential investment property usually lease it for many years, without experiencing corresponding decreases in rent amounts.

Increases in Value Due to Appreciation

Historically, real estate has shown to be an excellent source of profit due to the overall increase in investment property value over time. Of course, analysts cannot always predict real estate trends, which vary significantly across the United States.

Improving Your Investment Property - More Value at Sale

While it is providing cash flow, you can also improve your investment property to earn more profit should you choose to liquidate it. Upgrades to the appearance and functionality of an investment property can significantly increase its value. As trends and styles change, keeping the property interesting to renters can help you retain its value.

For a maximum return on investment, make note of improvements that actually increase a property's value. Installing energy efficient appliances and windows increases a property's value, as does by adding a bathroom and remodeling a room. Insulating a property also increases its value.

Inflation Is Your Friend When It Comes to Rent

Though your fixed mortgage payment will remain constant, inflation drives up home construction costs as well as rents. Population growth also creates housing demand and drives up rental prices when supply cannot keep pace.

Making Use of Equity

The equity in your investment property will increase as you pay down your mortgage. Though equity is usually determined when you sell a property, some real estate investors take out equity loans when interest rates and loan terms are favorable and use those funds for other real estate investment projects.

Find That "Steal of a Deal"

Finding a value-priced property is the most effective way to increase your net worth. Such deals aren't easy to come by, and savvy investors do their homework, browsing property listings frequently in order to quickly take advantage of opportunities when they arise.

Investors who wish to increase the value of their portfolio with real estate should also ensure that they have their financial ducks in a row. Good credit scores are a must, as is having the cash savings for the required downpayment -- usually 20 percent for investment loans.

35 REASONS TO INVEST IN REAL ESTATE

Bricks and mortar have taken a knocking in recent months – but it's still one of the most robust investment classes, especially in the long term. Here's why.

It's safe (as houses)

There's a reason why 'safe as houses' is a well-known phrase: it's true. According to research by AMP, Australian property has increased in value at a rate comparable to that of the share market since 1926 – an average of 11.4% per annum – despite a succession of wars, disasters, recessions and crises. It's done so without the volatility of the share market, too (more on this later), making it an all-round safer investment.

When you factor in the return and risk associated with buying property and shares, property wins hands down." "Shares have [marginally] higher capital growth, but the difference in risk is huge. The risk is measured in variation in returns and capital growth (or loss) on shares can range from +40% in a year to -40% in a week! You don't get that sort of variation in property, hence it is considered a safer investment."

It's easy to get started

You don't need specialist knowledge to start investing in property: in fact, many Australian property investors didn't start off intending to make their fortune through property. Instead, they just bought a house to live in. It's only after seeing the value of their home increase – and realising how much wealth you can generate – that many investors take the leap and start proactively investing.

It's easier to research than stocks and shares

Playing the stock market requires a lot of education. You have to understand how the system works, understand the complex world of trading (not least the different kinds of financial instruments used), as well as research brokers and fund managers. Once you've done this, you've then got to get to grips with the companies on the market – which involves trawling the financial press, annual reports, other company releases and so on.

Investing in property, meanwhile, is much simpler: at its most basic, you can simply jump online and start looking at properties. Admittedly, there's more to getting property investing right than just picking a property, but a significant amount of research can be done online (and is usually either free or inexpensive) or by visiting suburbs, open houses and auctions – without having to garner reams of specialist knowledge beforehand.

It's relatively easy to get finance

It may not feel like it when you're applying for a mortgage, but lenders like property. Home loans are a major part of any bank's business model, and lenders are more likely to lend on residential property than any other asset class – as evidenced by the fact that they will lend a higher proportion of the value (up to 95%) and at lower interest rates than any other asset class – including commercial property. This makes it a lot easier to borrow to invest in property than in any other asset class.

You can use leverage

Borrowing to invest in property also means you get greater access one of the oldest and most powerful tricks in the financial book: leverage.

"You can borrow more when using property as security as compared to using a share portfolio," explains Peter Koulizos.

Lenders will lend up to 95% of the value of the property, whereas they may only lend up to 50 or 60% of the value of a share portfolio. This greater borrowing power allows you to benefit from the capital growth of a larger asset.

"Imagine two people in the same job, on the same income, same assets and considered to be a similar risk by the bank." "The person wishing to buy a house may be able to borrow $450,000 based on their financial position whereas their workmate may only be able to borrow $300,000 to buy a portfolio of shares."

Assuming these both increase by 10% in a year, the person with the property has netted $45,000 in capital gain, while the shareholder has gained $30,000. That's a difference of $15,000 in just the first year – and remember, the profit's all yours.

Different strokes for different folks

Property is a remarkably flexible investment: no matter what your financial aims are, you should be able to find an investment strategy that suits you. Common strategies include:

Long-term capital growth

Looking to build a retirement nest egg? Long-term increase in value is the most effective way to do this.

"Property has historically proven its ability to deliver capital gain provided you select the right area with correct supply / demand ratio and demographics."

Positive cash flow

Need cash now? Choose properties where rents outweight holding costs.

"Certain property products offer exceptional cashflow. This extra money can definitely assist all areas of your life."

Adding value

Spotted a shabby old place with potential? You can renovate, subdivide or develop and create value out of thin air even through asimple paint job– unlike other asset classes.

"I can influence the value of my investment by renovating, developing or even altering the use," "However there isn't one thing I can possibly do to change the currency or share market. I can polish my wedding ring but the gold price still drops!"

100% control

If you invest in the sharemarket, you typically need to hire a broker to handle your trades for you, and the value of any shareholding is reliant on market conditions and the actions of the people running that company –introducing an element of uncertainty. This is much less the case in property: once you've settled, you directly own the asset and you have complete control over it (assuming you can keep up the mortgage repayments, and within the bounds of planning law). That's a hugely powerful thing, as it means that you can influence both asset worth (by adding value) and cash flow (e.g. by raising the rent) directly – something that's nigh-on impossible to do with shares in a company.

You can renovate (cosmetically)

Talking of influencing asset worth, there are a number of strategies you can use to do this, in ascending level of difficulty (and cost). One of the most common is cosmetic renovation – buying a tired property and sprucing up the interior and exterior. This can vary from simply repainting and putting in new carpets, to putting in new kitchens and/or bathrooms and landscaping gardens.

It's a tried and true method of increasing the value of a property – even the outlay of just a few thousand dollars can add twice as much to the right property.

The next step up from the cosmetic renovation is the structural renovation: adding bedrooms, bathrooms and so on. This is more complex than a simple cosmetic job –

with more scope for things to go wrong and costs to blow out – but can also be significantly more profitable.

You can subdivide

Find a property on a big enough block, in an area that's zoned correctly (or will be soon) and you can apply to the council to chop the block in two – and sell one or both halves for a tidy profit. While not physically difficult, finding the right property can be a challenge – and council approval to subdivide can take months.

You can develop

Biggest risk and biggest reward is taking an existing property or vacant block. subdividing and building upon it – usually units or townhouses. The profits can be substantial – if you can get it right.

Buying property that can later be developed can equal massive profits. These types of opportunities cannot be found in other asset classes.

An investment for every budget

A quick look at the property data in the back of this magazine shows that the too-often-made assertion that Australian property is unaffordable is simply untrue. Admittedly, if you're looking for an investment in the prime suburbs of Sydney or Melbourne, it's likely that you won't come away with much change from half a million – even for a two-bedroom unit – but middle-ring suburbs, regional towns and cities, or cheaper capitals (Adelaide and Hobart, for example) can all offer affordable entry points; if you buy smartly, you can also expect equivalent or even better growth than more expensive assets.

Price is flexible

If you buy a share, you buy it at the market price at that time: there's no scope to negotiate. In the property market, it's exactly the reverse: buying and selling is all about negotiation. You (or someone working for you) can talk down a vendor; equally, a motivated buyer could pay over the odds for the right property. There's also huge scope to find undervalued properties, particularly deceased estate or mortgagee sales, or sales due to divorce.

'an imperfect market'.

"As opposed to shares where all shares in the same company are sold at the same price and, in general, all the players in the market have similar knowledge, I can use my knowledge and contacts as well as my negotiation expertise to buy a property considerably below market price." "In the share market this type of knowledge would be considered insider trading and illegal."

It improves your financial knowhow

Perhaps a left-field advantage, but investing in property improves your financial know-how. The simple act of saving for a deposit teaches financial discipline; working the numbers in terms of affordability prior to purchase is essential, and once an investment has been acquired, the juggling act of dealing with holding costs, rental income and tax benefits not only requires some monetary dexterity, but also makes you more capable of managing your money – and making the most of every cent.

Tax breaks – negative gearing

Speaking of tax benefits, we'd be remiss not to highlight one of the most important benefits for investors: the fact that the tax office allows you to write off investment expenses against tax, thus lowering your income and your tax bill and offsetting any shortfall between rental income and holding costs either partially or in full. This makes investing in property more affordable for the everyday Australian.

Tax benefits – depreciation

As well as the negative gearing benefits, property investors also benefit from depreciation – the decline in value of the actual property, fixtures and fittings over several years. Depending on the age of the property and whether it's been renovated, this can run into thousands of dollars every years – and can be the difference between a property being negatively geared and paying for itself. Investors dismiss depreciation at their peril.

Tax benefits – CGT

That's not all, either. Property also benefits from a favourable environment in relation to capital gains tax: if you sell your own home, you don't pay any tax on the profit; meanwhile, if you sell an investment property that you've held for more than 12 months, you only pay capital gains tax on half of the profit. These three tax benefits mean that Australia has a uniquely favourable taxation environment for investing in property – and that's before you start looking at investing in property via super (more on that later) or targeted schemes like NRAS.

You can use your super

Self-managed super funds have been around for some time – however, it's only in recent years that investing in property via super has emerged as a feasible option due to changes in the law regarding borrowing. It's incredibly tax-effective: CGT on sale is just 10%, and zero if you're over 60; a recent ATO ruling also means you're now allowed to renovate properties held within the fund too. However, you do have to stay within the rules, which are quite complex, so seek advice before going down this route.

It's easier to hold onto if things go wrong

Margin calls are a common feature of shareholdings: essentially, if you've borrowed to invest in share, the margin call is when you are asked to deposit more money if the assets in your portfolio fall below a certain amount. However, it's almost unheard of for a lender to ask you to top up a mortgage if a property falls in value – as long as you can keep up the repayments, you'll be able to continue holding your property until its value increases again.

It's an asset you can use

Investment or not, your property is still just that – a property. So, should events take a turn which means you have to move into that property, you can (pending rental agreements, of course) whether for the short term or the long term – and, if things change again, you can move back out, leaving your investment intact. That's a hard thing to do with a share certificate or a bar of gold.

Not just investors in the market

An important factor in the robustness of the property market is that fact that it's not just investors buying and selling property – in fact, investors are the minority. Investors account for around 30% of all mortgages taken out (ABS, July 2011), with the remaining 70% by homeowners – who aren't necessarily buying with the principal aim of making money from property, but due to any number of reason. This provides the housing market with a base 'floor' of activity which, while not protecting it from ups and downs, does limit their impact somewhat.

"As long as people choose to live in houses, units & apartments, residential property will always be stable," comments developer Troy Harris. "From the young couple who have saved enough for a deposit, to the investor renting student accommodation through to the downsizer and retirement village, residential property is always sought after."

Limited immunity from fluctuation

Another experienced investor and market commentator, Margaret Lomas, argues that the right kind of property can also offer limited immunity against recession.

"During an economic slowdown, more demand from both buyers and tenants falls into lower markets." "[This increases] values and yields."

Other people pay for your investment

In fact, it's worth noting that, as well as being able to borrow the vast majority of the asset value and the tax benefits, you're also getting other people – namely tenants – to subsidise your investment through rental payments. You're getting three different parties helping you make money through capital gain (or cash flow) – making property one of the most affordable investments around.

The only thing Australians aren't taxed on

One especially for the homeowner, this:

"We get taxed on everything in Australia, but your own principal place of residence is one of the rare things left that the Australian government doesn't tax you on." "Therefore, you can add real value to your own home through a renovation or by redeveloping your property in another way – and every dollar of value you create is yours to keep. The taxman gets none of it."

Still keep growing – even when you're retired

Many investors following a capital growth strategy are putting together a nest egg for their retirement – whether that's based on selling down and creating a lump sum, partially selling down and living off rental income, or on living off a line of credit. However, what some investors forget is that, even after they retire in, say, 20 years, yield and value will continue to improve – making you worth more each year. Investors Direct chairman Bill Zheng also highlights that property investors are more likely to hold onto properties when they retire, due to the effort required to accumulate them.

It's a more stable investment

The property market is usually much less volatile than the share market, at least partly due to the effort required in order to purchase a property – in terms of due diligence, legal checks, inspections, length of settlement periods and so on. This means that property is less prone to short-term speculators than paper asset classes. This – along with the relatively long amount of time it takes to liquidate a property asset – also reduces market volatility significantly.

"Properties in well located area's, underpinned by good supply and demand, rarely crash overnight or even over extended periods of time." "They hold their own or at least level off and rarely experience major falls. Investors can avoid high risk areas simply by researching suburbs and properties well before they buy."

Bricks and mortar

Another factor which is comforting to many investors is that they've invested in something tangible – something they can 'look at and touch'.

"[Property is one of the few investments which you can actually see and feel, and this often makes it feel more real." "You can't take your friends for a drive on a sunny day past your share portfolio."

While much of this may be a psychological comfort, there's also a monetary benefit. After all, even if the worst happens, the fabric of the property and the land underneath will still have some tangible value – unlike shares in a company that's gone under.

The government's got your back

The government of the day – regardless of party - wants house prices to remain robust. Why? Because properties house voters.

"Governments naturally look after voters who own or rent houses, they therefore can't afford to upset them too much and are therefore unlikely to bring in legislation that adversely increases the cost of owning residential property." "Governments generally don't have similar concerns for shareholders or owners of commercial or industrial property."

Case in point: the last time negative gearing was tampered with was in 1987, when the government tried getting rid of it. The results were disastrous: investors stopped investing and rents in Sydney skyrocketed because investors didn't buy residential property. The decision was quickly reversed negative gearing was reintroduced.

Australia's economy is solid

There may be some short-term wobbles, but Australia's economic future is well and truly solid. The country's population is projected to reach at least 30.9m people by 2056 – and these people will all need housing, most likely in the state capitals. The resources boom – responsible for significant property price growth in parts of Western Australia and Queensland in particular – is also expected to continue well into the next few decades, with knock-on effects on supporting industries. This is all set to fuel solid property growth in the coming years – although savvy investors would do well to carry out extensive research into which areas will benefit most.

You benefit from other people's spending

Specifically, government and company investment. Spending on infrastructure like roads and rail and airports can boost values in a suburb or regional town which may have previously had accessibility issues; meanwhile,investment in new premises or projects –

universities, hospital factories, resources projects, shopping centres and so on – can provide employment opportunities and increase housing demand. New amenities can also see house prices increase, purely down to an area becoming a nicer place to live. And that all happens without you having to spend a cent.

Government incentives

On top of the relatively benign attitude towards homeowners, the tax benefits and the benefits property owners get from investment in infrastructure, the government will also directly give you money to buy certain types of property. The most well-known incentive is the $7,000 First Home Owners Grant, but most states also have some incentive for off-the-plan and new properties. Another investor-focused incentive scheme is the National Rental Affordability Scheme (NRAS), which sees investors paid over $9,000pa to invest in affordable housing.

Investors provide housing

Financial benefits not enough for you? Well, how about social benefits? Investing in property provides a supply of rental housing at a range of budget levels – meaning those that either can't or choose not to buy a property have a choice of places in which to live. Without property investors, providing rental housing would be solely down to the government – you're housing the nation.

You can pass it onto your kids

When thinking long-term for your investment, you don't just have to think your lifetime – you can also think about your children, too. Depending on the legal structure in which you own your properties, you can pass your investments onto your children either before or after you pass away. Sure, you can do this with shareholdings too, but how many top companies from 30 years ago are still at the top of the ASX 200? Not that many – whereas a well-positioned property should continue to grow over the long term.

You don't have to do the dirty work

If the idea of property hunting, renovating, developing, dealing with tenants or any of the associated tasks that come along with investing in property don't appeal to you, then you don't need to do them. The property industry is well-established, with the ability to outsource pretty much every task to an eager – and competent – service provider such as buyers agents, builders, property managers and so on. Sure, it may cost you – but the best providers also confer a competitive advantage which can actually boost your profits.

You can do the dirty work

On the other hand, if you do want to get hands-on with the process – whether that's researching properties, being an active landlord or renovating – then there's nothing stopping you either. As you've got control of your investment, you can be as involved or uninvolved as you wish or as is practical to your lifestyle. However, before plunging in head first, it's probably wise to make sure you've done the necessary research and preparation first!

3 MOST PROFITABLE TYPES OF REAL ESTATE INVESTMENT

Venturing into real estate investment is a decision you must never take lightly. It requires plenty of research before diving in, as well as patience and commitment. If done properly, investing in real estate will be a profitable journey. Moreover, it can provide a constant steady income and it is considered a warranty on financial and economic fluctuations. If you have already decided to try your luck in real estate investment, you would have already noticed the immense diversity found in the field. With endless options in front of you, it is difficult to decide which investment will be the most beneficial. As an investor, you are, of course, considering profit. It is important to invest in a property that yields a high return on investment. High return, however, does not always mean the highest rent.

In order to determine which property is best for you, you need to figure out how much you will make after deducting the amount you invested. Whether you choose to rent out the property or sell it, you will always be able to figure out an estimated profit. You can then compare your options and make the best real estate investment decision. Remember that you may not make a profit within the first few months of your investment. In the long run, however, you will find that real estate investment is a decision worth taking.

Now, if you are ready to invest, here are the 3 most profitable types of real estate investment.

1. Commercial Real Estate

A commercial space is definitely one of the most profitable types of real estate investment. There are many types of commercial spaces, including industrial, retail, office, and even parking spaces. Investing in a commercial space is generally expected to yield a high return on investment. Moreover, you will be renting to a business rather than an individual. This means the whole process will be smoother, as businesses tend to care about their image and will therefore properly manage the property. Furthermore, most businesses tend to pay rent on time, as they do not want to lose the space. If you find an opportunity to invest in a commercial space in a booming area, consider taking the prime real estate opportunity before it is too late.

2. Residential Rental Properties

Usually, a safe path to take, residential rental properties are a straightforward investment. If you invest in a residential property, you will be making money out of the monthly rent you receive from the tenant. In the long run, this can make a lot of money. You will also guarantee an income on a regular basis. However, you should keep in mind that the property will need regular maintenance to keep its value. Moreover, you might come across tenants who fail to pay on time or refuse to pay for any damage they have caused to the property. You may also be unable to rent out the property for a period of time. All these are obstacles that may affect the profit you make out of this investment. If for any reason, you decide to sell the property, you will probably profit from the sale. While most real estate properties are expected to see an increase in value, it is best to invest in an area that shows growth potential. This will almost guarantee that you are able to continually rent it out and even benefit from selling it if you decide to do so.

3. Fixer-Uppers

Bought with the purpose of re-selling, a fixer-upper is no easy task. This property is usually in a bad condition when purchased and bought for a relatively cheap price. The investor then fixes it and sells it for a profit. This type of investment is best for those who are looking to make money fast. However, keep in mind that this type of investment requires expert realty knowledge and intensive work. First of all, you will need to find an almost run-down property that shows great potential. Then, you will need to find easy and cheap fixes that will increase the property's value. Finally, you will have to market the property in order to make money out of the sale. Investing in a fixer-upper requires creativity, knowledge, and a lot of effort. If done correctly, this type of investment is guaranteed to make you profit in a relatively short period of time.

Which real estate investment is right for me?

Before you invest in any type of property, remember that you are not looking for the most rent, you are looking for the most profit. Making profit will depend on several factors, including the invested amount and the capital growth. Capital growth, or capital appreciation, is the amount your property increases or decreases in value over time. This means that you must consider the area you are investing in as well as the property itself. For example, investing in a studio apartment in a growing district may be more profitable than a five-bedroom villa in an area with no potential. The size of the property itself is not more important than other factors that contribute to its appreciation in value.

Ultimately, the best type of investment depends on what you are looking for. If you want to make quick money, maybe invest in a fixer-upper. If you are willing to wait, you can choose between a residential or commercial property. The decision will also be affected by how much money you have to invest. Regardless of the type of property you choose to invest in, always remember to study the market well. Conduct an analysis of the area and property to determine growth potential. You can also consult a professional if you require more knowledge before making your decision.

CONCLUSION

Any residential real estate investing deal that stands up under the scrutiny of this fundamentals-oriented lens, should keep your real estate portfolio and your pocketbook healthy, whether the residential real estate investing market goes up, down or sideways. However, if you can use the real estate market trends to give you a boost. The key is not to rely on any one "strategy" to try to give you outsized gains. Be realistic with your expectations and stick to the fundamentals. Buy property you can afford and plan to stay invested for the long haul. Whether you're a short-term or long-term investor, real estate investing can offer a lot of upsides. You must learn how to find great deals, how to evaluate a real estate investment, and how to finance any properties you want to buy. Additionally, you must treat it like a business and nurture it as it matures. It's likely not going to be totally passive up front, but as millions of individuals throughout history have discovered, the payoff is well worth the journey. The right real estate investments can result in monthly cash flow, asset price appreciation, and diversification, as well as tax benefits. You can learn how to invest in real estate by purchasing a fix-and-flip, a buy-and-hold or a vacation rental property.

www.ingramcontent.com/pod-product-compliance
Lightning Source LLC
Chambersburg PA
CBHW031416210526
45464CB00005B/1910